50 d

SET FORTH Y[OUR CASE]

Studies in Christian Apologetics

CLARK H. PINNOCK

THE CRAIG PRESS
Nutley, New Jersey 07110
1968

Printed in the United States of America

Copyright 1967
The Craig Press

Library of Congress Catalogue Number 67-29598

Ledell
Bailey

THE AUTHOR

Clark H. Pinnock, born in Toronto in 1937, received his B.A. degree in Ancient Near Eastern Studies from the University of Toronto in 1960, and his Ph.D. degree in New Testament studies from the University of Manchester in 1963. Prior to coming to New Orleans Baptist Theological Seminary in 1965, Dr. Pinnock was assistant lecturer in New Testament at the University of Manchester, serving under Professor F. F. Bruce. At the present time he is an associate professor of theology at New Orleans. His interest in Christian apologetics was quickened through close association with Dr. Francis A. Schaeffer at L'Abri Fellowship, Huémoz, Switzerland. Dr. Pinnock is the author of *A Defense of Biblical Infallibility.*

CONTENTS

INTRODUCTION

"It is one mark of the truth of our holy religion that it courts enquiry. Christianity lays open its claim to every one that asks a reason of the hope which it inspires, and declines no species of a fair investigation" (*The Evidence of Christianity*, Crocker and Brewster, p. 25). Thus wrote Daniel Wilson in 1829, before an antirational temper became dominant in our culture. The defense of the faith belongs to the preaching of the Gospel. Preaching without apologetics is scarcely preaching at all. It encourages naked credulity and shallow conviction. Christian and non-Christian alike demand to know, and have a *right* to know, that the historical and intellectual foundations beneath the Gospel are sound. In Isaiah 41:21, the Lord issues a ringing challenge to the false gods: "SET FORTH YOUR CASE, says the Lord; bring your proofs, says the king of Jacob." Certainly the Lord himself does not shrink from the demand for authenticating credentials on the part of the Gospel. Our Good News is an accredited claim and bona fide offer. Our confidence in its objective truth is reflected in our zeal for its defense and proclamation.

"Always be prepared to make a defense to any one who calls you to account for the hope that is in you, yet do it with gentleness and reverence" (I Peter 3:15). All Christians stand beneath this command, and many are disobedient to it. The earliest believers called men to an intelligent faith. They pressed boldly the claims of Jesus Christ as they had been dramatically verified in history by the fact of the Resurrection. Upon the validity of this historical datum rested and continues to rest the truth of the Christian message. In describing his witness, the Apostle Paul wrote of its two faces. "For we are the aroma of Christ to God among those who are being saved and among those who are perishing, to one a fragrance from death to death, to the other a fragrance from life to life" (II Cor. 2:15f). Our task includes Law and Gospel, a warning and an invitation, good news and bad, despair and hope. The negative side of the

1

coin consists in a radical unmasking of the natural man who is trapped in the prison of an impersonal universe, playing a role in a drama without a plot. The positive side involves a display of the total evidence which verifies and validates the Christian truth claim, together with a rebuttal of criticisms directed against it.

The shape of our defense is to some extent molded by the intellectual climate of our times. The apologist needs to be wise in his generation, and play the matter by ear. For there is no normative approach to Christian apologetics. Our aim requires a continual refocusing simply because our target moves ceaselessly. We have a responsibility to reach our generation. Although we may learn much from the wisdom of the ages, the moment fresh thought begins to wane, our witness becomes stale and irrelevant. This book has been written for believers in Christ who desire to witness intelligently and effectively for him, and who feel the heavy pressure from the current non-Christian consensus with its relativism and loss of absolutes, and, ironically, simultaneously from the existentialist theology with its fatal emphasis on subjective irrationalism.

The Christian Gospel pleases both heart and head. It is a rational and intelligent faith. Therefore, it cannot be presented on the spur of the moment without much reflective thought, in the spouting of prooftexts and an appeal to religious excitement in the soul. There is a need for more serious regard for the philosophical and factual structure of the Gospel, so that a bolder and more imaginative witness can be undertaken in this critical hour. May God grant a new Reformation in truth for the Church, and use this humble document to produce a substantial deepening in our understanding of the Christian faith.

It is an old saying that to steal from one writer is plagiarism, to steal from many is research, and to be inspired by any and all writers is creativity! Indebtedness could be acknowledged to many for the thoughts in this book, but must be directed to one, Dr. Francis A. Schaeffer, L'Abri Fellowship, Huémoz, Switzerland, a man valiant for truth. A mighty book requires a mighty theme. The grandeur of our theme is beyond dispute. Our prayer is that the book itself might lend glory to the Lord, and encourage the people of God to undertake a bold witness for him which will shake the foundations of our tottering, secular culture. May the Holy Spirit use the book to that end.

2

I

THE LEGITIMACY OF CHRISTIAN APOLOGETICS

Christian apologetics is concerned with a defense of the truthfulness of the Christian religion. The task of theology is to define the content of revealed truth, while the task of apologetics is to defend its validity. Theology and apologetics are twin members of a common family. In our spiritual warfare, the one is defensive, the other offensive. The aim of apologetics is not to trick a person into becoming a Christian against his will. It strives rather at laying the evidence for the Christian gospel before men in an intelligent fashion, so that they can make a meaningful commitment under the convicting power of the Holy Spirit. The heart cannot delight in what the mind rejects as false. Apologetics presents compelling reasons to the mind for receiving Christ as Savior into the total man. Faith is based upon credible evidence which people can recognize as trustworthy in accord with proper criteria for truth.

The Greek word *apologia* from which we derive apologetics occurs some eight times in the New Testament. It signifies a defense of conduct and procedure. Several times the Apostle Paul was called upon in a court of law to defend his right to preach the gospel in public (Acts 22:1; II Tim. 4:16). Festus made the sense clear when he told King Agrippa of his conviction that an accused prisoner deserves the right to make his *defense* in the presence of his accusers and in a court of law (Acts 25:16). The *apologia* Peter commands us to render (I Peter 3:15) is not primarily in the face of police enquiry; the verb "ask" rather suggests an informal question such as "Why are you a Christian?" To such a query every believer is obliged to be ready with a sensible answer. To assist in framing a convincing answer is the purpose of this book. Modern man is confronted by a bewildering array of clues to the meaning of the universe. Choosing Christ to be his ultimate clue is not an arbitrary act of desperation, but an intelligent step of faith based on good and

3

sufficient evidences. The aim of apologetics is to demonstrate the validity of the Christian system and defend it against attack.

However, the noble discipline of apologetics has fallen upon hard times recently. For its two implacable foes have reared their heads. On the one hand *Rationalism* has never left much room for supernatural revelation and miraculous Incarnation, and finds apologetics beneath its dignity. If the Christian faith consists merely of intuitive truths and ethical codes, to defend the case for supernatural Christianity is rather beside the point. On the other hand *Mysticism* with its delight in the empty irrationalism of the heart disdains apologetics as impertinent and unnecessary. Certainly the neo-orthodox theology would disown the term mystical to describe itself, but it is appropriate nonetheless for designating this facet of its thought. For the basic thesis of the dialectical theology is that the acts of God in history cannot be detected apart from a leap of faith, and the revealed words of God cannot ever be identified with any words. Divine acts are beyond history and divine words beyond language. Faith in Christ becomes an arbitrary act grounded in nothing. The gospel itself may be devoid of historical *fact* and objective *truth*, but this is no concern to "faith," so the new theology says. God might even be dead as some have alleged, and one could never be sure in the absence of any decisive proofs for his existence. Indeed the radical forms of the neo-orthodox theology are admirably suited to survive the death of God, because this word "god" describes only an existential relationship, and not the self-contained triune God of Scripture. A casual reading of the New Testament is enough to show how foreign to the gospel are these religious constructions. The very essence of the good news is the claim that in Christ Jesus God openly showed himself in the empirical realm of history, and on that basis he commands all men everywhere to repent (Jn. 1:14; I Jn. I:1-3; Acts 17:31). The Incarnation had a soteriological purpose— the name of Jesus saves, not the intuitive truths of reason—and it had an epistemological purpose—the "unknown God" is no longer unknown. There are checking procedures for testing the Christian clue, and it is the task of apologetics to present the fruits of them cogently.

Christian commitment does not take place in a vacuum. What modern unbelief needs is not less apologetics but more. Faith is *not* the opposite of knowledge. The scandal of the gospel is *not* its

4

alleged immunity from proof. The gospel makes sense, not non-sense. Its offense lies in its moral unmasking of the sinner, not in its supposed uncertain truthfulness. The mind is not to be left at the threshold in Christianity. Such deliberate irrationalism is positively anti-Christian and plays directly into the hands of unbelievers who cherish the illusion that the gospel is a foolish leap of faith. "The greater the risk, the greater the faith" is one of the most damaging fallacies ever to afflict the mind of Christian people. It leaves men secure in their false world views, and denies them access to the public evidences which make the gospel unique. Modern theology has rejected "magic" for "myth" and modern man will believe neither. The hour has struck for a virile apologetic which will challenge the naive confidence of humanism and display the beauty of the Christian system. We will never win a victory if we decline to enter the conflict. The current apologetic strategy of retreating from all positions under attack may avoid bloodshed, but can result only in abject surrender and total defeat.

Ironically enough, a definite species of irrationalism also appears in branches of Protestant orthodoxy. Because of an unbiblical appeal to the testimony of the Holy Spirit in the heart, an unholy alliance of sceptics and Christians together disparage the solid defences of the gospel. As if the faith which the Spirit commends to the heart must be an irrational faith! Is it not almost blasphemous, these Christians ask, to seek to make the gospel acceptable to the natural man? Can debate and argument ever really convert anyone? Does it not lead to endless wrangling and heresy?

This confusion arises through a failure to distinguish the inner from the outer testimony in the gospel. A Christian preacher or witness brings the data of Christ and his work to a person. Theology and apologetics join hands in performing this essential role in evangelism. However, apart from the work of the Spirit, the gospel will fall upon deaf ears. The problem lies in the inability of the natural man (I Cor. 2:14), not in the veracity of the gospel (II Cor. 4:3f). Conversion takes place when our witness to the truth, and the Spirit's creative work in the heart coincide (Acts 16:14). The inner and the outer witness are essential for nailing down certitude. The Spirit employs our witness as a *tool* in regenerating the heart (I Peter 1:23). The "foolishness" of the gospel (I Cor. 1:21) is not the offense it renders to the *ratio* (reason) of man, but to his

5

hubris (overweening pride). The gospel dissolves all his sand castles, and bursts all his balloons. But *in itself* the gospel is perfectly intelligible, consistent, and satisfying.

It is surely a delight as a Christian to reflect upon and appropriate the rich verities of Christian revelation. But at a certain point it is imperative to ask whether the grand assumption, Jesus Christ is Lord, is true or false, legitimate or fanciful. Theology-in-a-circle is an interesting intellectual pursuit no doubt, but has no compelling relevance to the world unless its subject matter is reliable. Obviously, Paul plants, Apollos waters, and God gives the increase (I Cor. 3:6). But it does not follow that the seed is not fertile and the water non-irrigating in its effects. In salvation the Spirit creates the *capacity* for receiving God's truth, but *truth* it is. In producing a photograph, light must fall upon the film, and the film must be processed to yield an impression. Both light and development are essential to a photograph. In precisely the same way the Spirit and evidences are essential to saving faith. To cite a telling phrase of B. B. Warfield,

> One might as well say that photography is independent of light, because no light can make an impression unless the plate is prepared to receive it. The Holy Spirit does not work a blind, an ungrounded faith in the heart. What is supplied by his creative energy in working faith is not a ready-made faith, rooted in nothing, and clinging without reason to its object; nor yet new grounds of belief in the object present; but just a new ability of the heart to respond to the grounds of faith, sufficient in themselves, already present to the understanding. We believe in Christ because it is rational to believe in him, not though it be irrational. For the birth of faith in the soul, it is *just as essential* (italics mine) that grounds of faith should be present to the mind as that the Giver of faith should act creatively upon the heart (*Apologetics* by F. R. Beattie, Richmond, 1903, p. 25).

Certainly the Bible teaches that the sinner is deaf, blind, and dead to the claims of the gospel. But this does not absolve us of the responsibility to present truth which can save under the power of the Holy Spirit (cf. Ezek. 37:1-14). What saves is the Spirit acting upon the data to bring about saving faith.

Psychologically there is no common ground between Christian and non-Christian, in that the latter will not yield to the force of

6

the evidence for the gospel, but will seek to equivocate its thrust. This fact does not relieve us of the duty of presenting it to him prayerfully. The Incarnation means that God has supplied data for his existence and character on which an intelligent faith commitment can be made. "These very works which I am doing, bear me witness that the Father has sent me," said Jesus (Jn. 5:36). The facts backing the Christian claim are not a special kind of religious fact. They are the cognitive, informational facts upon which all historical, legal, and ordinary decisions are based. Confidence in the factual truth of the gospel is simply logical incarnationalism. The fact of Christ can be shared with men without apology.

At the same time there is no place for arrogance and pride. Even the soundest apologetic has no power to make a man a Christian, or coerce a sinner to repent. The Spirit alone has the task of conviction to perform (Jn. 16:8f). But the conviction the Spirit engenders is itself grounded in evidence. The faith by which we shall overcome the world is anchored and rooted in the objective validity of God's acts and words. There is, however, no room for confidence in the flesh. The natural man has a deep-set bias against the gospel (Rom. 8:8). All our pleading and argument will do nothing to budge him from his usurped throne of self-worship. The gospel must be "caught" as well as "taught." Even where the soundest evidence conceivable is present to the mind, and faith follows (as with Peter in Mt. 16:16), it is no credit to human intelligence. "For flesh and blood has not revealed this to you, but my Father . . ." (v. 17). We are instruments in the Spirit's grasp. Without his skill no lasting results ensue. Yet, paradoxically, without the preacher and apologist the Spirit is silent (Rom. 10:14-17). The inner event originates with the Spirit, and the outer event originates with us. We are commanded to perform *our* task, not his, and this task includes Christian apologetics.

A sound grasp of Christian apologetics is an indispensable tool for evangelism. From philosopher to peasant the same questions are asked which differ only in the degree of sophistication. An intelligent Christian ought to be able to point up the flaws in a non-Christian position and to present facts and arguments which tell in favor of the gospel. The artist and the farmer have great need of Christ. If our apologetic prevents us from explaining the gospel to any person, it is an inadequate apologetic.

The need for apologetics has become more urgent with the rise of a monolithic secularism. It is a vanishing sector of people who can still be approached with prooftexts and historic Christian terminology. As the gap between the gospel and our culture widens, the bridges have to be longer and stronger. Apologetics deals in the area of *pre*-evangelism. A twenty minute sermon with three illustrations and a tearful invitation is simply insufficient grounds for requesting an intelligent decision for Christ. The total Christian understanding of the world, and the evidences on which it rests form a necessary deposit of knowledge which the Christian needs to master. Our problem does not stem from the insufficiency of gospel truth but from the increasing distance of unbelievers from it. Our situation calls for rugged conviction and boldness. Recent failure to bridge the gap between orthodoxy and modern agnosticism has been due to the sheer laziness of evangelicals to relate their treasure with intellectual courage to the questions being asked. Biblical truths are weapons in a spiritual warfare, and are capable of being wielded with great effect by a man of God. But they have grown rusty and dull for want of use.

Apologetics is related to worship too. It is always a joyous discovery to see afresh the adequacy and firmness of God's truth. Christian worship is far removed from the dark cathedrals, flickering candles, and mystical experiences. It arises in the soul fixed in adoration and contemplation of God's truth. Intelligibility is of the essence. The feeling that results from a tiring spiritual conflict in witness for Christ is not exultation in the flesh, but renewed amazement at the beauty of the good news!

Man has always been confronted by a cafeteria of clues to the meaning of the universe. His choice of the absolute ground of meaning, by which he orders the vast diversity of reality encountered, is a religious commitment. His problem is how to choose between the tempting alternatives. The discipline of Christian apologetics exists to assist him to see that the gospel of Jesus Christ is a live option; even more, that it alone can verify its claims, deliver him from despair, and provide solid ground beneath his feet.

8

II

THE BIG SELLOUT

There is a key that unlocks the door to an understanding of modern theology and explains current hostility to Christian apologetics. Once this structural principle is grasped, enormous light is shed on previously inscrutable problems of interpretation. Pitfalls and booby traps can be avoided with ease. The key is the "upper story" pattern in contemporary theology. By this device theology is calculated to survive even the "death of God" itself. But in actuality the price of this sellout is the complete demise of Christian apologetics.

In order to comprehend how theology moved into this position, two cultural facts must be carefully noted.

1. The Death of Hope and Romanticism

Basic to the humanistic mentality of Western man since the Renaissance has been the belief in the inherent goodness of man and inevitability of his progress. These grand assumptions have been shattered and widely abandoned because of the shocking revelations of man's inhumanity to man in the twentieth century, and the slow realization of the fundamental hopelessness of a naturalistic philosophy. Romanticism still survives in pockets of course, but the drift of our culture is in the other direction. This intellectual development of our times has created a crisis of meaning.

2. The Shift to Mysticism

In order to escape from the unpleasant implications of humanism which tend toward nihilism and despair, there has been a deliberate shift to a nonrational solution to the problem of meaning. The facts of history and the bleak logic of the non-Christian world view were found to strangle man's aspirations. So rather than surrender his *rationalism* (the ultimate autonomy of man's mind), man prefers to give up his *rationality* (his logical approach to things). Whereas his head cannot conceive an optimistic answer to his dilemma, his heart comes across with an intuition that saves the day. He *knows* this accidental collocation of atoms we call a world has no meaning, yet he chooses to *believe* in a meaning he creates for himself. The prominence of the existential mood today is only explicable on the basis that it allows man to have logical absurdity without any stigma.

The greatest single tragedy in modern theology is the failure to challenge this secular shift to irrationalism at its foundations. Instead theology has largely moved in exactly the same direction. It too has accepted the unthinkable, namely, a divided field of knowledge with mystical intuition as the clue to reality.

The Divided Field of Knowledge

UPPER STORY

The non-rational, non-logical, paradoxical, symbolic, untestable, unverifiable, suprahistorical, imaginative, surreal

---

Impenetrable Concrete Slab

LOWER STORY

The rational, logical, historical, factual, real, testable, verifiable, empirical, provable, scientific.

The "lower story," according to the new theology, is the realm of cause and effect, where man confronts brute facts in their great plurality, and functions logically and rationally. This realm is supposed to yield no meaning, no ultimate clue to things. It is necessary to go upstairs for meaning, to the "upper story." The upper level is the field of intuition, faith, and conjecture. It is in no way related to or connected with the lower level. It is a state of non-mind, the region of the nonrational mystical experience into which LSD users escape with considerable relief. For it enables people to stamp out reality as it is actually experienced and substitute a cerebral paradise of one's own creation. Instead of challenging our culture with the distinctive feature of the gospel, namely its objective historical base (Jn. 1:14), modern theology has jumped on the bandwagon on its way to a fool's paradise.

Let us pause to consider a few examples briefly of how the upper story theology works. Basically the subject who has faith becomes all-important, while the object of his faith is rather inconsequential. The person of Jesus, for example, is known as a contemporary symbol, embodying some ideal he is supposed to epitomize, but insofar as he is considered a historical individual, his identity is shrouded in deep darkness. In the lower story, historical criticism is said to yield only a human prophet who preached the end of the world; while by an upper story leap of faith it is possible to raise him to divine significance. By this device it becomes possible to identify "Christ" with whatever modern ideal we wish. For the Nazi theologians (e.g., Kittel and Hirsch) the Christ was indistinguishable from the force of social change found in national socialism. Because liberal theology gave up the standard of historical revelation it became prey to a satanic Christ. The confession "Jesus Christ is Lord" has come to mean almost nothing in our day because of the upper story mentality.

The same pattern is easily discernible in the approach to Scripture in the "new theology" (viz., the theology which espouses a divided field of knowledge). The Bible is placed in the lower story—a victim of scientific criticism, and yielding no evidence of its divinity. The "word of God" is put in the upper story—a non-verbal, non-rational, mystical, non-communicative "revelation." The "encounter with God" takes place, we are told, in the upper story. As a human document, the Bible is fallible and errant; as a medium of "revelation" it is inspired. As much could be said for the Koran, Shakespeare, and *Das Kapital*. No weight is given to the uniquely revelatory character of Scripture in the teachings of Jesus and his apostles. But by this neat device, a person can retain the scepticism

11

of a Strauss in one part of his brain (the lower story), and the faith of a Luther in the other. And if anyone catches on to what you are doing, the cover up trick is to turn pious. Simply identify reason with works, and the empty imagination with faith, and your critic will go away! By the death of such noble terms, Satan has won many a battle.

The upper story device applies to many other areas of Christian doctrine. In the doctrine of creation, the method is to put all the Biblical teaching upstairs in the region of "faith." By this means, the theologian can jump on the bandwagon of whatever the current scientific consensus happens to be, and appear terribly enlightened. At the same time, creation comes to mean "this is how *I* see the universe." No heads are bumped, a concordat is worked out with the scientist, and everyone gets prizes! Meanwhile the biblical teaching about the origin of things goes unnoticed and unheeded.

Biblical miracles can be neatly side-stepped using this device. The miracle occurs in the *seeing* of faith, not in the *fact* of history. A miracle is the interpretation which believing people gave to an event which touched them deeply. Israel made a lucky escape from the delta of Egypt, and cried "Yahweh!" The word for god served to satisfy their desire to express their gratitude. But nothing happened that would shock the naturalist. The water from the rock, the quails, the manna, crossing the sea of reeds—all these are put down to "faith." The miracles of the Bible do not prove God exists as they claim to, but merely that people *believed* he did. Again the upper story device protects the new theologian from all criticism from the side of historical and scientific fact. If the modern secular universities ever decide to eliminate their departments of religion, it will not be because they believe in the supernatural, but because their whole stance is irrationalistic and offensive to the demands of an empirical age.

A theologian who is quick on his feet can manage to dodge almost every objection that has ever been hurled against the Christian faith by taking refuge in the upper story. Take the resurrection of Christ, for example. By faith we confess that God raised Jesus from the dead. This faith is taken to be an upper story commitment, barring any possible testing procedures. This means, in effect, that the event was not "public," and that, if a reporter from the *Jerusalem Post* had been covering the event of the resurrection, he would have

12

detected no irregularities in the death and burial of Jesus. Indeed, according to the new theology, belief in the resurrection is the province of the psychiatrist (why did the disciples believe it?) rather than the historian (what really happened?). Resurrection is an upper story belief. There is no way to know whether it happened or not, save by believing it did.

The upper story enables a theologian to talk about the fallenness of man without believing in a literal Adam. The "fall" is put upstairs, in the area of "meaning," and Adam is left downstairs, in the shrouded world of fact and truth. Again a Christian doctrine is detached from the world of factuality and rationality, and isolated in the sealed capsule of arbitrary faith. The upper story symbols are in no way subject to verification or falsification, and their content is not fixed. The subject who has faith simply loads these symbols with the meaning he chooses in accord with the secular mood of his day. The Cross is an example of a contentless symbol in the new theology. The Cross is a constant theme, but the blood is never mentioned except in scorn. All the "theories" of atonement are put downstairs. What precisely Jesus did for us is not explained. The Cross means whatever the interpreter wants it to mean. If he can extract its meaning from the Bible in some way, so much the better, but, if he cannot, nothing is lost. For it is the contemporary Christ who saves, they say. The Cross can mean anything from love to hate, from humility to a toasted cheese sandwich. The same goes for the deity of Christ. His divine names, Lord, Son of God, Son of Man, are given emotional value, without metaphysical significance. These are taken to be upper story designations, terms which express someone's ultimate reference point, or the things of highest value to him. The doctrine of the Trinity in the upper story theology becomes purely a metaphorical description of God produced by men who saw redemptive history that way. If we attempt to take it as literally true, it becomes a mathematical absurdity due to the failure to interpret the Bible existentially. The Bible believing Christian has never been confronted by so clever a device before. But, if he will take the time to master this divided field of knowledge trick, he will find himself in a good position to counter it.

The upper story pattern in theology has only recently come to prominence, but it is by no means new. It. has deep roots in European theology since the Renaissance. Lessing preferred inner certainty over the relative uncertainty of historical events. Theologians have been trying to jump over Lessing's "ugly ditch" ever since. Kant made the dichotomy between faith and reason, between the noumenal and the phenomenal worlds, and thrust a thick wedge between religion and reality. Kierkegaard made the antithesis very explicit, by sharply opposing faith and reason. He is most directly responsible for the new theology, but is not its only architect. Oddly enough the new theology with its upper story is a child of *both* rationalism and existentialism, insofar as both movements dislike history. They dislike it also for much the same reason; namely because historical fact is not sufficiently certain enough to support faith. From that point the two movements separate, rationalism moving into scientific humanism, and existentialism moving into the upper story pattern. But both reject the Biblical claim that what God did in history *is* a sufficient ground for decision and faith. It is anti-biblical to insulate the gospel from the acid baths of historical criticism. It can stand the investigation, providing the prejudices are left at home. This dichotomy between faith and fact is fatal to Christianity and opposed to the entire Biblical witness. It is time it was exposed once and for all as a cul de sac.

The upper story in modern theology is diabolically clever. The layman should not be surprised if theology often seems to him ambiguous and ambivalent. For the first time in history theology has taken ambiguity into the heart of its system. The upper story is a sophisticated way of retaining the the Christian symbols, while at the same time denying them content and verifiability. The secular humanist can find refuge in this pseudo gospel without ever relinquishing his hold on his naturalism. The new theology is effective in the churches, because it manipulates cynically the Christian symbols which are deeply rooted in the memory of the people, and subtly empties them of all definable content. The congregation has already lost its power before it comes to realize, if it ever does, just what has happened, for when X is a symbol for Y, and Y a symbol for Z, and Z a symbol for X—things do become rather hard to follow! The big sellout in modern theology comes at the point of the complete elimination of the sovereignty of God. His existence is hidden and shadowy; his saving acts are concealed and equivocal; his revelation is subjective and ambiguous; his Christ is an elusive phantom; his laws are open to amendment; his Word is subject to

14

error. God is made to be impotent, unable to command men to repent on the basis of powerful arguments (Acts 17:31), capable only of peeking out from the curtains offstage, hoping some will respond. When this line of thought is taken to its logical conclusions, it seems apparent that the word "God" is only a word. It stands for a certain subjective state in man. God is a relationship, nothing more. Man feels the need for meaning, and cries "God," but he never can know until the end of his days whether this "God" is really there. It is equally possible that no god is there. The upper story route in contemporary theology is a dead end street. It leads as surely to despair as naturalism does. Only the road is longer getting there. Classical liberalism was a dangerous but easily detectible foe of historic Christianity. But the new theology is a slippery customer and has managed to come up with a closer counterfeit of the gospel. It is on that account more dangerous.

The effect of the upper story in theology is the complete destruction of apologetics and evidences. There is left absolutely no way to challenge the non-Christian to receive Jesus Christ. Theology has been converted to *solipsism*, the view that reality is whatever the individual makes it. The three descending steps to the abyss are clear: first, subjectivism (religion is all the way you see it), second, relativism (it doesn't matter how you see it), and third, agnosticism (no one has the answer). Solipsism is a nice way to describe modern theology. Insanity is appropriate but less kind. Whatever we call it, the new theology can lead us nowhere, and we had better find a different route.

III

THE RADICAL UNMASKING

One of the best kept secrets from the public at large in the twentieth century has been the death of hope and the loss of the human. From every direction, from painting, music, literature, theatre, films, an avalanche of testimony has been building up announcing grimly man's agonizing dilemma in this post-Nietzschean epoch of the decomposition of his gods. In Christian apologetics as in theology, the Law is preached before the Gospel, in order that the unregenerate man be exposed and unmasked before the demands of a holy God, and directed to the road of grace. The wicked are like chaff (Ps. 1:4-6), they have no valid starting point for their thinking (Prov. 1:7), and the foundation of their habitation is sand (Mt. 7:26). No flesh can boast in the presence of God (I Cor. 1:29; Rom. 3:19f). Indeed the emperor in the ancient legend, despite all of his pomposity and pride, had no clothes. So it is with modern man if he continues to by-pass the redemption which is in Christ Jesus.

In this latter third of the twentieth century, it is apparent that the once proud dogmas of optimistic humanism are dead and buried. Belief in the inevitability of progress and the innate goodness of man has been replaced by a mood of cynicism and despair. Oswald Spengler wrote: "Mankind has no aim, no idea, no plan, any more than a family of butterflies or orchids." History is endlessly repetitious, having neither progress nor ultimate goal. Spengler's melancholy was shared by two fellow historians, H. G. Wells and Edward Gibbon. In 1939, near the close of his life, a disillusioned Wells wrote:

> There is no creed, no way of life left in the world at all, that really meets the need of the time . . . there is no reason whatever to believe that the order of nature has any greater bias in favour of man than it had in favour of the ichthyosaur or the

16

pterodactyl. In spite of all my desperation to a brave looking optimism, I perceive that now the universe is bored with him, is turning a hard face to him, and I see him being carried less and less intelligently and more and more rapidly, suffering as every ill-adapted creature must suffer in gross and detail, along the stream of fate, to degradation, suffering and death.

Gibbon came to much the same conclusion when he admitted that history is "little more than the register of the crimes, follies and misfortunes of mankind."

The root problem of the non-Christian humanist is the sheer pointlessness of existing in a godless world. The director of the British Humanist Association, H. J. Blackham, admitted that "the most drastic objection to humanism is that it is too bad to be true." Bertrand Russell summed it up with characteristic eloquence:

> That man is the product of causes which had no prevision of the end they were achieving; that his origin, his growth, his hopes and fears, his loves and his beliefs, are but the outcome of accidental collocations of atoms; that no fire, no heroism, no intensity of thought and feeling, can preserve an individual life beyond the grave; that all the labour of the ages, all the devotion, all the inspiration, all the noonday brightness of human genius, are destined to extinction in the vast death of the solar system, and that the whole temple of Man's achievement must inevitably be buried beneath the debris of a universe in ruins—all these things, if not quite beyond dispute, are yet so nearly certain, that no philosophy which rejects them can hope to stand. Only within the scaffolding of these truths, only on the firm foundation of unyielding despair, can the soul's habitation henceforth be safely built (*A Free Man's Worship*, 1918).

Testimonies of this kind from non-Christians awakening to the logic of their own position could be added from an unnumbered host—from Sartre, Camus, Heidegger, Durant, Voltaire, Strauss and many more. The unbounded optimism of Western man has reached exhaustion, and he faces his own extinction in his own manufactured hell.

This despair is vividly portrayed in the writings of Franz Kafka. In his novels and short stories Kafka gives literary expression to the philosophy of Friedrich Nietzsche. Kafka is a modern man. His gods have disappeared and his men are dying. His foothold in reality is based upon the conviction that there is no foothold possible.

17

In all his work, *The Castle, The Trial, America,* anguish and ambiguity are at the heart of things. The future is always bleak, impenetrable, and menacing. A heavy pall of sadness hangs over everything. He leaves his reader alone, in the cold, black, wintry night. The senseless fatality of his characters is rooted in the empty futility which life in a godless world must inherit. Kafka knows no dancing at the tomb of God. He turns aside and weeps.

This sense of metaphysical despair receives a full exposition in the "theatre of the absurd" movement. This group of playwrights, including Samuel Beckett, Eugene Ionesco, Harold Pinter, and Jean Genet, has dedicated itself to depicting the absolute emptiness of life. They achieve this aim by employing an effective technique— the use of nonsense language. By dramatically altering the structure of normal language and syntax, these writers create an *experience* of absurdity in the audience. The "absurd" may be defined as the disparity seen between the world as it actually is and the world as it was hoped to be. The clock of hope has run down. Without his metaphysical roots, non-Christian man is effectively lost and drained of the purpose to live. He is an accidental scrap of life surrounded by death. Instead of arguing for the meaninglessness of man's existence, these writers simply *present* it. The breakdown of language in *Waiting for Godot* or *The Bald Soprano,* for example, is intended to indicate the breakdown in all significant existence and communication. At the root of man's existence is nothingness. Man's dreams are in wreckage and ruin. There are no exits from the non-Christian world. Life is a dead end street. The theatre has become an eloquent vehicle for presenting today's dilemma. Beckett reveals his trapped position in these words:

> How am I, an a-temporal being imprisoned in time and space, to escape from my imprisonment, when I know that outside space and time lies Nothing, and that I, in the ultimate depths of my reality, am Nothing also? (See Richard Coe, *Samuel Beckett,* Grove, 1964, p. 18).

Artistic expression is given to man's hopelessness by Francis Bacon, one of Britain's leading painters. His major theme is the sheer horror of existence. His canvases are full of screaming people, prison cages, and gory slabs of beef. From his own admission, Bacon paints man "in the hell of his situation." The artist himself is addicted to gambling and did his finest work in a drunken state. Desperation is written all over his life and work. Yet he illustrates the truth of the Scripture, "without Christ, without hope."

William Golding captures an aspect of this mood in *Lord of the Flies*. A group of plane-wrecked British schoolboys stranded on an island (boat-shaped to symbolize the journey of life) completely shatter the myth of human innocence. We all live east of Eden. The fig leaves of man's pretensions to uprightness and nobility are torn away. In the mirror of this play we see our evil and our guilt, and the sight of it merely augments the problem.

Modern man has experienced a rude awakening. There is a recognition of something terribly wrong. These testimonies are not the opinions of pathological pessimists. These spokesmen are intellectual leaders of our culture. Today's prophets are secular.

The factors causing the death of hope are not at all mysterious. The illness began the day man placed all his confidence in himself. Since that day he has been living on borrowed capital, and today his resources are almost completely exhausted. Two factors are sufficient to explain his current bankruptcy.

1. The Intrinsic Logic of His Position

The dilemma of modern humanism can be explained with terrifying simplicity. Matter plus time plus chance equals zero! If man is the illegitimate offspring of a thoughtless parent order, the mockery of fortuitous chance, his significance is nil. There is no conceivable way to construct a meaningful dwelling for man upon the uncongenial foundations of chaos and accident. Modern man has simply come to realize the logical implications of his foolish autonomy and is beginning to pay the price. Sartre was right, this fact *ought* to give him nausea. The further man moves toward epistemological self-consciousness as a non-Christian, the closer he will come to nihilism and despair. The more consistent, the less happy. The equation of naturalism is simple, but devastating.

2. Man's Inhumanity to Man

Alfred Lord Tennyson saw man moving forward and upward, working out the beast, and letting ape and tiger die. But that was the nineteenth century. The beast in man refused to die. Instead he grew larger. The optimistic hope for the educated, moral man

19

of tomorrow never crystallized. The heart is deceitful above all things, and desperately corrupt" (Jer. 17:9). Whereas it was once ridiculed, the doctrine of original sin is again respected as an essential insight into human nature. Before any humanistic utopia can be reached, a transformation in the human factor must be made. A possibility of this exists in the New Being of the gospel, but little hope remains outside its boundaries. Man is at the end of his tether. The facts of history discourage him, and the logic of naturalism crushes him. A cry goes up to heaven, "How long?"

The death *of* hope leads directly to the hope *for* death. For man still cherishing his ideals, death is an enemy. But to him whose life is pointless, death is a sweet savior. Hemingway embraced it as his messiah. Camus named suicide as the only truly serious philosophical problem. Death, without further possibility of good or evil, is preferable to life without hope. The set of choices is admittedly a bleak one, but it is all the choice the non-Christian has left. Preoccupation with death is a distinguishing mark of our time. The "death of God" controversy ought to be set in its proper context. Our era at the same time glorifies and hates death. Its prominence in Freud, Heidegger, Kafka, and Bacon is a sure sign of a collapsing culture. A philosophy of life which does not make its terms with death cannot hope to survive. For most people it is a topic as distasteful to discuss as it is impossible to evade. Yet it is the source of the deepest anguish in the human breast. Death, a fall into a bottomless void, strikes fear to the heart. Modern man is fast approaching the place where he hates life and fears death. His only hope lies with Him who can extract the sting from death, and grant a more abundant life.

The rising curve of contemporary secularism has almost reached the point of complete cynicism. From this point the line may turn in a parabola to a new basis for hope, either in a new mysticism grounded in the creative imagination (the existential way), or back to the historical Christian faith, on which foundation a durable cultural edifice could be constructed. Victor Hugo wrote, "There is nothing so powerful in all the world as an idea whose time has come." It is surely the time for a vigorous restatement of the Christian faith in the firm confidence that its restoration to the basis of our culture would lead our nation to health and vigor again.

The radical unmasking required today cannot be done by evangelicals who are culturally barren, however. Where there is no serious interest in literature and the arts, there can be no effective communication of the gospel to our contemporaries at large. Each Christian does not need to be a literary critic himself, but his ears ought to be attuned to the sound of his world, and the Christian community should be a place in which these interests are encouraged, not shunned. In general Christians are culturally uninformed; much like the man who, when asked if he had purchased the new Random House Dictionary of the English Language, replied, "I'm waiting for the film version." Until we stop relying on instant-culture, the abbreviated book and the weekly digest, the task of effective evangelism will not get done. Cultural and spiritual growth *are* related. The enlarged capacity created by an appetite for a wider spectrum of cultural interest will increase our intake ability for spiritual truth too.

It is sadly ironical that those best acquainted with our culture seldom have answers to its dilemmas, while those with the answer hide their treasure behind barricades of ignorance. The Christian life ought to exhibit richness, not poverty. Only thus can we hope to penetrate the defenses of those who perish through want of a vision. Our generation will not be impressed with the language of Zion, the mouthing of empty cliches. If we hope to change our culture, we will have to change our lives, and take the gospel seriously. A clear demonstration of the existence of God is called for in every sector of life and culture. It is lacking in so much of contemporary American churchianity.

IV

STAMP OUT REALITY!

The escape route from despair is a flight from reason. The older humanist was rational in methodology, and naturalistic in premises. But the new humanist, instead of recognizing his *naturalism* to be the root of the whole problem, turns away from rationality itself. The explanation is simple: the only way to avoid the impasse of naturalism without bowing to God is to slay the dragon reason. For irrationality is preferable in non-Christian thought to either logical despair or rational theism. Having lost their confidence in the world of reality, the artist, playwright, poet, and the theologian have retreated into the area of nonrational, subjective, personal experience. "Faith" becomes the magical wand which transforms despair, based on logical considerations, into hope based on the creative imagination. Metaphysical despair is the unavoidable axiom of a godless philosophy. Reality becomes an enormous steel trap, an inhuman prison, mocking man's dreams and aspirations. The revolt against reason, the characteristic mental attitude of our age, has religious roots, and is directed against the *Logos,* Jesus Christ, who created all things by the word of his power (Jn. 1:3; Heb. 1:3). It is the denial of God's structure in order to replace it with a man-centered structure.

The popularity of Albert Camus among the beatnik, the New Left, and the avant garde artistic movements is understandable in the light of the passion to smash reason. The late Algerian playwright had a brilliant sense of the tragic in life. He bares his heart in *The Plague, The Outsider,* and *The Myth of Sisyphus.* Life is futile and purposeless. His answer is absurd joy in the face of unspeakable suffering and death, a pathetic irrational wish that reality be different than it appears in his godless system. Jean Paul Sartre travels the same path. The two great ontological human experiences are anxiety and nausea. They reveal the absurdity at the base of all

22

existence. But Sartre cannot live consistently with his philosophy. He can find meaning only by going against it. He was quoted as saying, "Man is absurd, but he must grimly act *as if* he were not." In other words, the non-Christian must live in pretense, against the logic of his own position. Atheists exist like Sartre, but consistent ones do not. Atheism is more on the lip than in the life. A world truly absurd contains nothing but chaos. It is without values, rationality, hope. Not the grimmest existentialist lives in a world like this.

For over a century, the Huxley family have been famous for their naturalistic humanism. Aldous Huxley began his career as a sceptic of all absolute values. But in his closing years in Southern California, he evolved a philosophy of hope based on a mescalin drug experience. When "tuned in" Huxley received "a mystic awareness of the richness of bare being," a "goodness encompassing good and bad." Although Huxley thought his life was crowned by this mystic discovery, his shift from rationality to this nonrational drug mysticism actually indicated the bankruptcy of naturalism in the Huxley family. The delight his brother Julian finds in Teilhard de Chardin, the mystical Catholic Darwinian, is evidence of the same flight from reason. Humanism is too bad to be true. All the labor expended in human causes seems rather futile where no goal is in view. How can one justify life in a meaningless universe? The non-Christian answer is to move up into its own version of the "upper story," the realm of dream and illusion, where perchance hope can be recovered through a mystical leap of faith. Carl F. H. Henry was fully justified in writing:

> The whole frame of reference within which modern man seeks the meaning of life and the solution of his persistent problems, displays its inadequacies in test after test (*The Drift of Western Thought*, Eerdmans, 1951, p. 12).

The short circuit to hopelessness brought on by the logic of naturalism is provided by a mystical, and essentially religious, leap of faith. Julian Huxley saw the need for a religion without revelation. That is, a religion that would give cozy warmth of undefined symbols, without the interference of a God who actually exists. Thus Huxley himself manipulates lofty symbols like "destiny," "values," "shared responsibility," "evolutionary goals," etc., in order to cover up the apparent void created by his own system. Out of nothingness only nothingness can come. A logical locomotive will not stop just because someone screams. Huxley's integrity is in real doubt. Having set the train in motion, he now leaps off as the precipice approaches, and hides behind the ancient oak of mysticism. Not a very impressive end to a century of rationalism.

The movement of Western thought toward the East is apparent in all of this. The growing popularity of Zen Buddhism among the cultural avant garde in America is due to its deliberate irrationality. In Zen, reason (*vijnana*) and the intuition (*prajna*) are always in contrast. Mystical subjectivism belongs properly to the East, not to Christianity. The Zen master Professor Suzuki correctly rebukes certain Christian mystics who erase the creature-Creator distinction, the transcendence of God over the world. For historic Christianity based on the Bible is not the home of mysticism and irrational faith. The current attempt to link up Eastern mysticism with Western theism (e.g., Altizer) is an example of pure wishful thinking. It is *Zen* which gives irrationalism its proper home, the repudiation of true meaning for aesthetics and intuition. In Zen, the individual can excuse himself from all responsibility, and withdraw into a contemplation of his navel. Man, reason, and culture—all are dead.

The retreat from reason into the subjective realm can be traced on every side of our culture. The new turn in Martin Heidegger's thought from his earlier analysis of the ontological significance of man's feeling states, to his recent interest in the poet Hölderin and the prophetic meaning of poetry is an example. The visionary grasps intuitively the shape of being, and gives it expression in the poetic word, a "revelation" of Being in language. Heidegger escapes from the real, palpable world in which by logic he can find no answer. By attaching himself to poetic intuition and making the poet his priest, he aspires to overcome the discomfort of a rational world. The action painting of Jackson Pollack and the chance music of John Cage fit into the same category. By a repudiation of all rational controls, both men hope to create meaningful forms by the operation of *chance*, the ultimate spring of all creativity to them. (Bacon's addiction to gambling needs to be viewed in this light.) Similarly the sex-mysticism of Terry Southern or Henry Miller is a desperate attempt to launch oneself into a mystical orbit, where hopefully some answers to life's enigmas can be encountered.

But undoubtedly the clearest example of the retreat from reason is found at the *psychedelicatessen*. If the desire is to manipulate contentless symbols which give the appearance of communication without challenging naturalism, then LSD and its family of hallucogenic drugs is without question the sacrament of the movement. For it enables the devotee to move onto the "upper story" with incredible ease. Drugs create a heightened self-awareness, and a mystical sensation of being united with Nature. All the senses are expanded and jumbled. Color can be tasted and sound smelled. The aim is to *disorient* the mind, so that the individual can detach himself from the real world and commune with the Beyond. Salvation is a coin-operated electric Kool-Aid machine! The drug can propel you into Nirvana *now*; so why wait? The conversion of Timothy Leary to Hinduism is hardly surprising. Religion in the East is beyond intellect and conviction. It is a world of nondiscrimination and nondifferentiation. The great irony in the eastward movement of the West is the belief that this trend is a *forward* step. Millennia ago men in the East lost all hope for rational answers and opted for mystical pantheism, a decision which produced the immobile giants of Eastern culture. At the same time the decision destroyed the basis for initiative, thrift, purpose, and vitality.

The drug experiment is a part of the "exploration of inner space," the attempt to locate *within* the soul a clue to meaning which has not been discovered *outside* it. On the evolutionary view that religions are the product of human development rather than its explanation, psychedelic drugs can be useful in re-creating the myths of ancient people in order to use them as a medicine for modern psychoses. Simply by going on a trip a person, according to Professor Pahnke, can enjoy a conversion like St. Paul's. Possibly enough LSD might even produce a resurrection appearance! Modern man worships at the shrine of the unconscious and looks to biochemistry for a savior. It is however a great *delusion*. LSD will convince a person of powers he does *not* have, and answers he does *not* possess. In real life, the Captain Marvel who leaps from the window of a skyscraper is dead. The drug taker has two choices: a one-way ticket to an asylum, or a shelf in the deep freeze for spiritual dropouts. Neither a bad trip nor a good trip can secure what a man really needs, namely, a Creator and Savior who is really *there*. The drug movement is a desperate attempt to find meaning in a world where none exists apart from Jesus Christ. It is a pure escape from life which has become unbearable. LSD only gives the illusion of adding to one's stock of answers. The salvation that cannot save a sober man is unlikely to save an intoxicated one. Leary's dictum—"it becomes necessary to go out of our minds in order to use our heads"— is a counsel of despair, a salvation by self-destruction. Only the abnormal can find this blessedness. It is only the gospel which speaks to the *total* man today.

The resemblance of the LSD solution to the mentality of the "upper story" theology cannot have escaped notice. Each is moving away from a rational answer toward a nonrational existential religious experience without content. Salvation is reached through a "final experience." In theology, the drugs may be employed in order to speed up the manipulation of symbols, as in recent experiments at Boston University, where divinity students tuned in to a deeper meditation on Good Friday with the aid of the "sacrament," But there are other ways of turning on. The dramatic rise of occurrences of tongue-speaking fits into this picture too. Release from anxiety can be obtained by letting the mind go free to the accompaniment of soft babblings from the throat. The appearance of the "gift" at Notre Dame, and its results, a greater love for the Mass and the Rosary ought to alert thoughtful Protestants to the extreme dangers implicit in the movement, simply because of its wider context, the widespread retreat from all rational controls. Biblical Christianity is rooted in historical (I Cor. 15:14) and rational truth (I Jn. 4:3). Drugs only mess up the genuine believer, because his worship is based on objective truth, not dreams or myths. A "trip" is as likely to open the individual to demonic invasion as it is to edify him.

The real threat of the retreat from reason in whatever form it may take is its implications for world religion and world government, two treasured goals of international liberalism. The new emphasis on mystic feelings has softened our generation up for the imprinting of whatever worldview the rulers of tomorrow may wish to impose. The perfect instrument is now ready for the ultimate Ruler in an omnicompetent and omnipotent State to herd the human population into the barns of his choosing. The current openness of leading Marxist intellectuals to a dialogue with Christians stems less from a true softening on their part than from a realization that

26

the new theology in Protestant circles contains nothing that Communism needs to fear. For a religion rooted in the social gospel, which thinks of man primarily in terms of mass social and political forces, is an ally, rather than an enemy of Marxism. A grand political-religious collusion of the kind pictured in Revelation chapter 13 and 17 is certainly within the realm of possibility in the near future. In George Orwell's *1984*, all history was a palimpsest, scraped clean and reinscribed exactly as often as was necessary. Whenever the interpretation of history and fact becomes an arbitrary subjective decision, mankind is subjected to a totalitarian ideology. History becomes the servant in the hands of the regime, and a tool of social engineering. It spells the death of the individual and the culture. But this is precisely the direction in which we are presently moving, away from reason and history, into the horrors of subjective existentialism. The Nazi movement has given the world a horrible object lesson when a world view is detached from historical fact. The myths become autonomous and destructive. The Christian faith is rooted in the *real*. It bases its claims on historical events. It is altogether opposed to the contemporary intellectual climate.

V

THE BREAKING POINT

Romanticism is the procedure of giving an optimistic answer to the human dilemma without a sufficient base for so doing. From the Christian point of view, the death of hope and romanticism was a beneficial thing. Romanticism is an enemy of the gospel because it lulls people into a false security. The avant garde artist may be unpleasant, but he is at least rather honest. Mantovani's music is more anti-Christian than Samuel Beckett's plays simply because it drugs the non-Christian into peaceful slumber, when he ought to be awakened to the existence of a real problem—his life and destiny. A sensitive believer can only feel deep agony in his heart in the realization that the last pocket of romanticism to die is right inside the bourgeois Church itself. Almost unconsciously, religious people regard the middle-class non-Christian resident of a lily white suburb as nicer, more polite and thrifty, cleaner and kinder. But according to the Biblical faith, it is the *godly*, not the *good*, who will be saved (Gal. 2:16). Moralism without the Christian base is a one way ticket to hell. American Sunday School humanism is a menace to Christianity. The gospel is theism, not moralism. The "nice behavior equals nice times" mentality is at the root of why we are losing our children to secularism. Romanticism must die before the gospel can be taken seriously. Everyone has watched the late show in which the hero gets the girl, the villain is apprehended, and everybody lives happily afterward. Far from being a "Christian film," this kind of idealism is a *lie*. The great merit of the most radical novelist today is that at least he is not complacent. The death of romanticism is a *good* thing for the gospel. Our culture has moved so far toward nihilism that the two leading artists who are called humanists, Francis Bacon and Alberto Giacommetti (because they depict human subjects), actually paint so gloomy a picture of life

28

that they would have been scorned a century ago by the humanists of that day.

There is not a single art form which does not bear the scars of the death of romanticism. As men realize the logical implications of their unbelief they move gradually and irresistibly toward the breaking point, steadily losing a grip on their humanity, and finding themselves unable to operate in the real world. In philosophy, for example, serious grappling with ultimate questions of life and death has almost vanished, replaced by word-games and language analysis. With the loss of absolutes since Hegel, in which the distinction between true and false, right and wrong, breaks down, the philosopher is virtually out of a job. Or, one need only trace the sad history of art in the past hundred years, from impressionism to cubism, to dada, to surrealism, to pop, to op, to psychedelic art. The exercise can bring sadness to the person who treasured the culture which the Reformation produced. In the same manner there is more significance in the scrapings of John Cage and Karlheinz Stockhausen than merely the invention of electric oscillators. Something has died in music—perhaps music itself. Bach wrote to the glory of Jesus. Cage writes out of homage to Chance. That the products should differ ought scarcely to surprise us. Certainly the phenomenon of the absurd, in theatre, in poetry, in novel, and in the Happenings, ought to awaken us all to the desperate plight of modern man.

The longer men dwell in the prison of naturalism, the closer the parallels become between the freeman and the inmate of a real penitentiary. Samuel Beckett was quite nervous before the performance of his play *Waiting for Godot* at San Quentin prison before an audience of some 1,400 prisoners. How would they receive the sophisticated and symbolic play, he asked himself. They loved it! For the simple reason that the world Becket describes, in which every non-Christian lives, is a prison, and the inmates recognized it at once. The absurd world of Samuel Beckett is not a whit more attractive than the gray existence of a penal institution. The immediate and distant horizon is bleak. There is nothing to compensate for the effort of living. The individual is a number, merged into the herd, without independent value or significance. Upon release, he is helpless to fend for himself because personal convictions have rotted away. There are no foundations left to build upon.

29

Each culture and every individual exists somewhere on the line of despair and has an individual breaking point. With the advance of the non-Christian ethos in Western civilization there will be increasing consistency in the application to all areas of life of the naturalistic premises. The more consistent a person is in putting the non-Christian position into practice, the more evident it will become to him and others what it really means to be a non-Christian. Man is in the process of self-destruction in the twentieth century. The speed at which he reaches his breaking point is determined by the degree of epistemological self-awareness he exhibits. He must learn to live honestly without God and Christ, without continuing to borrow from the capital of divine revelation and redemption. Neo-paganism in the post-Christian era must inevitably become a lot poorer before it will fabricate riches of its own. Seldom has this fact been better expressed than by Rushdoony:

> Wherever man asserts his independence of God, saying in effect, that, while he will deny God, he will not deny life, nor its relationships, values, society, its sciences and art, he is involved in contradiction. It is an impossibility for man to deny God and still to have law and order, justice, science, anything, apart from God. The more man and society depart from God, the more they depart from all reality, the more they are caught in the net of self-contradiction and self-frustration, the more they are involved in the will to destruction and the love of death (Prov. 8:36). For man to turn his back on God, therefore, is to turn towards death; it involves ultimately the renunciation of every aspect of life.

> To deny God, man must ultimately deny that there is any law, or reality. The full implications of this were seen in the last century by two profound thinkers, one a Christian, the other a non-Christian. Nietsche recognized fully that every atheist is an unwilling believer to the extent that he has any element of justice or order in his life, to the very extent that he is even alive and enjoys life. In his earlier writings, Nietsche first attempted the creation of another set of standards and values, affirming life for a time, until he concluded that he could not affirm life itself, nor give it any meaning, any value, apart from God. Thus Nietzsche's ultimate counsel was suicide; only then, can we truly deny God, and, in his own life, this brilliant thinker, one of the clearest in his description of modern Christianity and the contemporary issue, did in effect commit a kind of psychic suicide. The same concept was powerfully

developed by Dostoyevsky, particularly in *The Possessed*, or, more literally, the Demon Possessed. Kirilov, a thoroughly Nietzschean character, is very much concerned with denying God, asserting that he himself is God, and that man does not need God. But at every point, Kirilov finds that no standard or structure in reality can be affirmed without ultimately asserting God, that no value can be asserted without being ultimately derived from the triune God. As a result, Kirilov committed suicide as the only apparently practical way of denying God and affirming himself, for to be alive was to affirm this ontological deity in some fashion (*Intellectual Schizophrenia*, Presbyterian and Reformed, 1961, p. 25f).

There is at the present time then, a radical disintegration of the non-Christian man as he reaps the harvest produced by the seed he has sown. After many years the crop is approaching full maturity, and the ingathering is proving a most unpleasant time. He has laid up treasures on the earth, the sphere of his ultimate values, the place of his only reward and enjoyment. His values are dead on the vine, being merely the dictates of social and personal convenience. The ethic of evolution, the survival of the fittest, has yet to take its full toll. The world has still to see the full maturing of de Sade's "natural behaviour" based on the principle of "what is" is right." The simple equation—matter plus time plus chance—has yet to yield its full horror.

However, a man does not exist who does not fall short of total consistency. Each non-Christian holds to a mixed world view. It is impossible to live inside his system logically, so he borrows liberally from gospel capital, on his own terms of course. He loves what the gospel can give him (rationality, significance, pardon, identity), but will not part with his autonomy and hence must steal from the Christian system to survive. The more consistent he is with himself, the closer he draws to the breaking point. Having first discarded God, he tends to jettison anything which smacks of association with God, which, as he finds in the end, is everything worth having. Therefore, he stalls his engine on the line of despair in the attempt to avoid either distasteful termination, salvation under God or despair in a naturalistic prison house. Every non-Christian inhabits a half-way house somewhere in his experience. Hugh Hefner, the ingenious juggler of American symbols, is noted for his advocacy of unlimited sexual license. However, in a recent interview, Hefner

31

admitted his distaste for a woman who actually put his philosophy into effect. Furthermore, when asked whether he would encourage his daughter to be promiscuous, he admitted his intellectual schizophrenia: ". . . intellectually I may think in a certain way; practically I may act in another way. I am and I remain a combination of incoherences that I uselessly try to reject." Hefner does not admit the logic of his position because he is unwilling to face a world with the philosophy he espouses! At least in his lover and his daughter he retains a sector of sanity and morality. But it is not to his credit. It only proves the basic dishonesty of the non-Christian position.

It has been observed in the life of a prison, that whereas a prisoner may regard no private property outside the prison sacred, very often he would under no circumstances steal from a fellow prisoner. Though he may profess a world without moral absolutes, he would on no condition squeal on a fellow prisoner. In every man there are moral motions which he can no more eradicate than fly. These are rather to his condemnation than to his credit, but they do expose the point of contact for the glorious gospel of Christ. The good news calls man back to the living God, the fountain of all rationality, love, significance, morality, and freedom. It urges him to forsake his rebellion which only yields him irrationality, absurdity, silence, and despair, and to accept the Christian set of presuppositions within which life is possible. There is a danger implicit here. If you take away man's lie, you may be taking away his hope. So the Christian witness needs to act gently and in love, lest the person he seeks to win should bolt to the point of total breakdown. Unmasking the natural man is the dark side of apologetics, but a needful part. The mask must first come off if man is to see himself as he is.

The cultural point of contact for the gospel lies deep within man himself, as one created in the image of God. The inner contradiction needs to be sought out and located, so that the balm of Gilead may be applied. A person can profess disbelief in gravity, but living consistently with that profession is quite another matter. There are more atheists in lip than there are in life. In his day Jonathan Edwards sought to destroy false happiness by presenting the reality of hell and judgment. We must seek to destroy that spurious security too by whatever tool at our disposal. Starting where man is, it is our duty to inform him of his inconsistency, and at the same time both nudge him to the logic of his own position and urge him to the logic of ours. The tin roof of his hastily constructed shack must be ripped off so that the harsh elements of the real world might awaken him to his folly and stimulate him to seek Jesus Christ.

VI

OUR MONOLITHIC CULTURE

Traditionally and officially America is *pluralistic* in religion. Diverse convictions are held honorably and freely throughout the land, and no sect is allowed an establishment over the rest. The common bond which held the original states together was Christian culture, but each region was to practice her version without interference from the federal power. The intent of the first amendment to the American constitution was not the creation of a secular state, but the imposing of a check on the central government from coercing the states in this matter. At the present time, however, because of the decline of Christian faith and the effectiveness of mass media, America is rapidly becoming a *monolithic* culture with uniform religious characteristics. The various cult functionaries serve a general religion of humanity and the American way of life. A striking parallel with the Roman Empire is pointed up by Gibbon:

> The various modes of worship which prevailed in the Roman world were all considered by the people as equally true; by the philosopher as equally false; and by the magistrate as equally useful. And thus toleration produced not only mutual indulgence, but even religious concord (Cited by Peter L. Berger, *The Noise of Solemn Assemblies*, Doubleday, 1961, p. 68).

Humanism is as much a religion as Christianity, though it is not called one. It is nonetheless the religion of the land both within the churches and without. Biblical Christianity is being pushed aside from every sector of life—science, education, welfare, government, psychology, theology—and most people proceed with scarcely a glance at it. The country at large, the polls tell us, professes a brand of religion in surprising numbers, but the people clearly believe in the *practical* irrelevance of the gospel. At a speed which is quite amazing the nation is being conditioned to a naturalistic way of thinking, the denial of all absolutes, and the relativism of all con-

34

victions. There are characteristics of the new emerging culture which no thinking person should ignore.

One of the necessary myths of a monolithic culture is the myth of neutrality. Because Man is the ultimate standard by which all things are to be measured, he is expected to approach questions of values and religion with a godlike objectivity. Strong convictions are equivalent to prejudices, firm principles to a bias. Although the politician appeals to sectional interests in order to get elected to office, the last thing in the world he must do when installed is to admit any sectional interests. Though people vote for their own self-interest, their elected officials pretend to stand for the common good while practicing brazen political deals under the table. In religion the myth of neutrality is widespread. All the creeds are equally grand—none true. Leaders speak of our Protestant-Catholic-Jewish heritage, as if such a hyphenated monstrosity really meant something. (If the hippies have their way, we shall soon have to attach Zen to that designation.) It is nice to have convictions, so long as you don't believe they are true! In this context a real Christian, who believes the name of Jesus is the only name under heaven capable of saving (Acts 4:12), is an unreconstructed bigot. He knows, however, with the proverb, "the one who says he is not prejudiced is a liar," that this neutrality is destructive and false. The proper procedure is to have the courage of your prejudices! Man according to the Bible is set in a particular culture and approaches reality with a religious set of categories to which he has committed himself. The man who pretends a lofty neutrality above the mass of men is more vulnerable to human sins than the person who admits his perspective and respects the viewpoints of others. The new citizen, friendly to all convictions, but attached to none, is a menace. The trend can only issue in the destruction of all values.

A monolithic culture tends to level values to the lowest common denominator to avoid unpleasant division and strife among men. Firm convictions are a threat because they divide men who share them from those who do not. Hence in a monolithic culture only the beliefs held in common are absolute. If prayer in the State school offends 4% of the pupils, none should engage. in it. If 10% of the students prefer homosexual to heterosexual relations, equal time must be given to teaching both sides. The pupils learn that "values" are important for life, but also that no way exists for knowing which values. Many are convinced that Albert Schweitzer's ideas were higher than Himmler's, but since both were carried out sincerely, it is difficult to explain the basis for such a preference. The only really sacred thing in a monolithic culture is social harmony. Convictions which divide men ought to be kept private and not be allowed to intrude in the public sector. This virtual "erosion of the mind," an avalanche of facts without a hermeneutic, leads directly to the disintegration of a culture. The loss of identity, the incapacity for action, the frustrated violence, the painful rootlessness of our day, all trace back to the relativism of humanism. We hear of antireligious conditioning in the Soviet schools, and find security in the costly myth that our own schools are neutral. Yet, it is almost the expected thing for a Christian coming to the university to find his beliefs attacked unmercifully by zealous faculty members who see it as their messianic task to wipe his mind clean of all inherited ideas and implant within it the one conviction, that there are no absolutes. Conviction beyond that is a crime. Bland humanism is the key to advancement. The anesthesia of culture the goal. Relativism is moral and intellectual atrophy. It results in the destruction of genuine morality (for inhumanity is a way of life too), and of freedom (for human "rights" become arbitrarily defined by the divine State). It is the direct antithesis of the gospel which claims universal validity and application to all men.

The faith of our monolithic culture which is emerging is the religion of humanity. The happiness of man is the single tenet, and whatever is human is sacred. The way of salvation is through the restructuring of the social environment and results in the satisfaction of the desires of all men. To achieve the goal of universal happiness, however, it is first necessary to remove all discriminatory legislation and prohibitions. Revolution and freedom are the key words. A law which restricts the freedom of some groups causes pain to them and is unfairly discriminatory. The "civil rights" movement for the homosexual is already in full swing thanks to the Mattachine Society, the Wofendon Report, and the ecumenical Council for Religion and the Homosexual. The cry for freedom is a cry for anarchy, the destruction of all revealed law and its replacement by a fluid set of humanly appointed rules. *Vox populi* equals *vox dei*. Man is holy. The most lurid display of perversion and sadism is culturally significant. Whatever is, is right. At last the philosophy of Marquis de Sade may win the day.

The religion of humanity forbids any absolutes. Doctrinal convictions discriminate against unbelievers. Taking the gospel to the Jews, for example, is an anti-Semitic act, because it introduces an antithesis into society. The refusal to pray with a Unitarian minister is interpreted as sheer bigotry in the context of the religion of humanity, for which the only inviolable credo is "In Man We Trust."

In order to deal effectively with this generation for Christ, it is imperative to detect the shape of this humanistic culture. Let us select three areas in which the new mentality is deeply ingrained already, government, education, and science.

In the biblical understanding, the State is a necessary evil. There is no sociological form in a fallen world without force. The State is an emergency measure instituted by God to suppress evil which constantly threatens to overwhelm the world. The eras of greatest misery to the human race are those in which governmental power is broken altogether. However, the Bible does not think of the State *messianically* either. It too requires restraint to keep it from becoming an antichrist. The framers of the American constitution were aware of human nature, and provided for checks and balances in the system, whereby the power would be widely distributed and not accumulate in the hands of a few. The humanistic view of the State is totally different. It is a human invention, designed to lead mankind to Paradise on earth. If the citizens would hand over their incomes, their lands, and their resources to the beneficent State, the latter would reward them bountifully. Socialism or collectivism is the political system of humanism. The State is the domestic and international Savior. "From each according to his ability, to each according to his need." The divine State provides cradle to the grave security, and asks only the total ownership of country and people. From the Biblical viewpoint, however, blind confidence in the omnicompetent Sate is disastrous. Political charity is no charity at all! The concentration of power in the hands of a few men can only work us ill. Government is not a Santa Claus. It is not the source of any of the goods it grandly bestows on the people. Everything it gives to the people it has first taken from the people. The current

37

move towards collectivism in America is based on a humanistic view of man, his nature and problems, and we may all live to regret it.

Education has become the property of the State in America, and increasingly of the federal power. In the Bible, education is the duty of the *home*. Believing parents are admonished to rear their children as a sacred trust from God and in his fear and worship (Deut. 6:7; Prov. 22:6; Eph. 6:4). It is their fundamental covenantal duty. In the early years of American history education was handled locally, in line with the ideals of parents and community. But with the rise to prominence of the public schools, responsibility for the child's education shifted from parent to State. The children effectively became the property of the State, under its influence and jurisdiction, for a large part of the week, and for the formative years of their lives. It became then the aim of liberal humanism to use education in the conditioning of society into a monolithic culture. The primary aim of education was to be the social adjustment of children into a group oriented mentality. This involved the elimination from the curriculum of beliefs and values not universally held. The education became child-centered, not content-centered, and stressed self-development, rather than his learning of the wisdom of the past. Statist education is becoming a major threat to the Church in America. As it becomes increasingly secularist and humanistic, Christian parents will come to realize how impossible it is to raise their children in the Christian faith while throwing them to the wolves in their education. Education may prove to be the point at which the drift towards collectivism is stopped. The striking increase in Christian schools across the country may arrest the growth of Statism and the monolithic culture.

Science means one thing to the expert practitioners in various fields, and quite another to the general public which is subject to the propaganda of scientism. Science is a sacred cow, and one of its most persistent myths in the twentieth century is the nebulous concept, "Evolution." Christians are constantly asked whether they "believe" it, as if the word conveyed anything specific. It is always easier to detect the myths of other people than to discern one's own. The myth of Evolution is so entwined in the current world view that its absurdities are seldom even noticed. It ought to be apparent to the casual observer of the history of science since Darwin, that the theory he propounded, far from becoming better established, is become shakier with every passing year. If you ignore for a moment the brainwashing of magazines with a *Time-Life* mentality, and listen to the experts in the various fields, you would soon realize that the data on which this grand hypothesis depends are slender indeed, and capable of a dozen different constructions. The *fact* is that the basic requirement, the spontaneous origin of life, has never been observed or demonstrated, and in the light of probabilities and the laws of thermodynamics, is a most unlikely hypothesis. The reason Evolution is believed and taught as fact is not due to the evidence for it, but rather due to the *need* for it. Any "natural miracle" (that inert matter is creative) is preferable to a humanist over a "supernatural miracle" (that God is the Creator). The State schools do everything they can to promote the myth because it is essential to the religion of humanity. Man cannot be autonomous if there exists a transcendent God with a divine Law. Such a God must die. Evolution is accepted because it shuts Him out, and leaves man free. But what an awful freedom! The freedom to know nothing, to be nothing, to believe nothing. The words of Paul have never been more fitting in the history of the world than now: ". . . claiming to be wise, they became fools . . ." (Rom. 1:22).

The only absolute in our monolithic culture is that there are no absolutes; the only belief that all beliefs are relative. One thing is right, that which seems good in your own eyes, and one thing holy, humanity. The philosophical significance of pornography in our day is the concerted attempt to use it in the breakup of all standards. By debauchery of every kind it is hoped to transcend all antithesis, and achieve "freedom." By a return to chaos, from whence all has sprung, salvation is being sought. God is dead. Only man and his caretaker State remain. All differentiation in truth and morals is swallowed up. A mystical pantheism is all that remains. All the colors shade into one another. Man is lost in hopelessness. His is the integration into the void.

VII

VALIDATING THE GOSPEL

In the wake of a radical unmasking, the Sun of Righteousness appears all the brighter in its splendor. But it is insufficient merely to show another position is faulty and untrue unless it can also be shown that the Gospel itself is well founded. It is not enough that the Christian faith should be pragmatically true or personally rewarding unless its substance can stand the test of rigorous investigation. Validation is the task of Christian evidences, an important subsection of apologetics. Myths and fables are immune to historical research and analysis, but the Christian message is open to examination. Apologetics takes the *incarnation* just as seriously as theology does. Both are centered in Christ. His advent and ministry provide both the redemptive content and the epistemological grounding of our faith. The Christian faith is an intelligent faith. Apologetics is concerned to provide evidence that the ground on which the structure rests is firm.

Ideally our approach to the question of validation should arise from Biblical data. Upon examination it appears that the Scripture provides a broad hint concerning the shape of our defense of the faith. In both Old and New Testaments the same pattern emerges: that divine revelation is accompanied by supernatural indicia, namely, prophecy (supernatural knowledge) and miracle (supernatural power). These accompany the acts of God and his prophetic words.

In the Old Testament the true prophet may be identified by the test of whether what he predicts actually comes to pass (Dt. 18:21f). One of the distinguishing characteristics of the Living God over against the false gods was his capacity to announce the future beforehand (Is. 41:21-24; 42:9; 45:21; 46:11). His ability through his spokesmen to transcend the alphabet of human knowledge provided objective proof of his sovereignty over history.

In the New Testament Jesus repeatedly predicts his crucifixion and its outcome in the Resurrection. This was to be the ultimate sign which he would provide men with (Jn. 2:18-21). At the Resurrection two miracles meet: his predictions are fulfilled (Mk. 8:31), and God's power is demonstrated (Rom. 1:4).

In the Old Testament the existence of God is established by an appeal to historical evidence. Moses was worried that Israel would not listen to his words from God. To counteract the incredulity of the people Moses was given the gift of miracle working (Exod. 4:1ff). After the mighty hand of God had been seen in the miraculous timing of the Red Sea miracle, Israel believed anew in the Lord's power (Exod. 14:30f). At a later date God asked Moses: "How long will they not believe in me, *in spite of* all the signs that I have wrought among them?" (Numb. 14:11). Rahab came to faith in the Lord when she encountered good and sufficient evidence for the reality of Israel's God (Josh. 2:8-11). Gideon's doubts were quieted by divine signs capable of overcoming his hesitation to act (Jdg. 6:13,17, 37,40). On Mount Carmel the prophet Elijah called for a great confrontation with the prophets of Baal (I Kings 18). "The God who answers by fire, he is God!" In reply to Elijah's faith the Lord acted, and in the miracle demonstrated his existence and power for all the people.

In the New Testament, Jesus Christ appears on the scene making tremendous claims for himself. His lofty teachings concerning his own deity were authenticated by the performance of miraculous signs. The Gospel of Mark is replete with examples of the evidential value of miracles (Mk. 1:28,45; 2:10; 5:19,42f; 6:2,14; 7:37; 8:18-21, etc.). The Gospel of John is pre-eminently the Gospel of Signs. After the miracle at Cana his disciples believed on him (2:11). Upon the healing of his son, the official believed in Jesus (4:53). "These very works which I am doing bear me witness that the Father has sent me" (5:36). When the people saw the miracle of feeding the five thousand, they recognized Jesus to be the Prophet, the Messianic King (6:14f). Jesus performed so many signs that the people had a dilemma: "When the Christ appears, will he do more signs than this man has done?" (7:31). The raising of Lazarus from the dead caused many to believe on Jesus (11:45), and goes far to explain why so large a crowd gathered at his triumphal entry (12:9-12,18). "If I had not done among them the works which no one else did, they would not have sin; but now they have *seen*

41

and hated both me and my Father" (15:24). Thomas brings the Gospel to its theological finale in his confession to Jesus, "My Lord and my God!" (20:28). But he came to this conviction after receiving objective proof that Jesus had indeed risen as the disciples had said. "Now Jesus did many other signs in the presence of his disciples, which are not written in this book; but these are written that you may believe that Jesus is the Christ, the Son of God, and that believing you may have life in his name" (20:30f).

The miracles of Christ provided men with a powerful incentive to trust him. "Even though you do not believe *me*, believe the *works*, that you may know and understand that the Father is in me" (Jn. 10:38). In another situation Jesus chided the cities of Chorazin and Bethsaida for not believing on the basis of good and sufficient evidences. "For if the mighty works done in you had been done in Tyre and Sidon, they would have repented long ago in sackcloth and ashes" (Mt. 11:21). Conversely, when John the Baptist was perplexed about the identity of Jesus, his attention was drawn to the miracles Jesus performed as evidence of the dawning of the Messianic age. "Go and tell John what you have seen and heard!" (Lk. 7:22). In the early apostolic preaching too an appeal was made to the mighty acts of Jesus which accredited his divinity (Acts 2:22; 10:38). In like vein Paul told King Agrippa that he had no excuse for his agnosticism. "For I am persuaded that none of these things has escaped his notice, for this was not done in a corner" (Acts 26:26). Confirmatory signs also accompanied the ministry of the Apostles. (Heb. 2:4). "The signs of a true apostle were performed among you in all patience, with signs and wonders and mighty works" (II Cor. 12:12).

But undoubtedly the greatest stress in the New Testament is placed on the bodily resurrection of Jesus Christ as *the* supreme sign of the truth of the Gospel. Jesus presented himself alive after his suffering to the disciples "with many infallible proofs" (Acts 1:3). His resurrection was an attested fact of history (Acts 2:32; 10:41; I Cor. 15:3-11). It was the supreme demonstration of the deity of Jesus Christ (Rom. 1:4). It provided mankind with an evidence of universal validity (Acts 17:31). "If Christ has not been raised, then our preaching is in vain and your faith is in vain" (I Cor. 15:14). We have a living hope *because* God raised up Jesus (I Pt.

1:3). The existential cart must remain *behind* the historical horse and not intrude in front.

This survey of biblical data assures us that an historical approach to Christian evidences is valid. There are doubtless other ways of proceeding, but this way enjoys clear Biblical support. The primary basis of apologetics is the historical *datum* of the Incarnation itself. The good news is not a fairy tale. It is grounded in objective events. Jesus has presented himself as divine Messiah, and the resurrection has dramatically authenticated his claims. In this age of the non-rational existential experience it is imperative to stress the fact that the gospel is about God's acting in the *empirical realm*. For the validation of the Christian claim we make our appeal to history.

It is important to pause here and consider the relation of Christian evidences to the work of the Holy Spirit. For obviously the mere existence of the Scriptures or historical evidences do not of themselves create saving faith nor impart illumination automatically. An effective witness for Christ included two elements: the outer testimony to the gospel and the inner testimony to its truth. The human side to evangelism is indispensable. "How are they to believe in him of whom they have never heard?" (Rom. 10:14). This witness is to be convinced and convincing. Our evidences are a part of the total proclamation. The object of faith has substance. Yet unless the sovereign Spirit employs our witness as his tool and creates the *capacity* for a saving response (cf. Acts 16:14), our word will fall upon cold hearts. The inner witness of the Holy Spirit is essential to genuine faith (Rom. 8:15; I Thess. 1:5), but the truth he attests is nonetheless *truth*. Because we cannot do everything, does not imply we are to do nothing. Our task is to present the data about Jesus. Our effectiveness is of God's good pleasure (I Cor. 3:6).

A typical reaction from the new theologians to this concept of apologetics is shock that faith be in any way made dependent upon the uncertainty of historical research. The Christian claim is, however, firmly grounded in history. If God has not revealed himself unmistakably in human history, the incarnation was a failure because that was its intention. Ninety percent of the uncertainty alleged is due to a naturalistic methodology applied to the historical data, reflecting an antisupernatural bias, rather than to any actual ob-

43

scurity in the facts. One can be a historian without being a positivistic historian!

That the gospel rests upon an objective historical foundation is a priceless asset in this world in which there is a cafeteria of clues as to the meaning of the universe. The basis on which we rest our defense of the gospel consists of evidence open to *all* investigators. The non-Christian has no right to disregard the gospel because it is a matter of "faith" in the modern sense. On the contrary it is a matter of *fact*. The historical foundations of the gospel, especially the resurrection itself, comprise a powerful incentive and challenge to our secular contemporaries to consider Christ and his claims on their lives.

A parable will illustrate the dilemmas of nonverifiable religious assertions in contrast to the gospel. It is told by John W. Montgomery.

> A little green man eating toasted cheese sandwiches is sitting on a planet exactly two miles out of the range of the best telescope on earth. He is a figure who loves us, particularly if we eat toasted cheese sandwiches. He has a nasty habit of moving out of the range of the telescopes as they increase their range (*The Altizer-Montgomery Dialogue*, Inter-Varsity Press, 1967, p. 67f).

The credibility of a religious claim rests upon its ability to verify its terms. If the data central to the message remains hidden to all investigation, suspicion arises about its existence. A religious claim without any way to test it out is as meaningless as a nuclear test ban treaty without adequate checks. The experimental method of religious experience has grave disadvantages as we shall see in the next chapter. If there is no way to check out the validity of the historical gospel, there are no criteria for distinguishing the Christs of Steiner, Swedenborg, and Mary Baker Eddy. The beauty of the gospel in the avalanche of competing religious claims is precisely the possibility we have of checking it out historically and factually.

The intent of Christian apologetics and evidences is not to coerce people to accept the Christian faith, but to make it possible for them to do so intelligently. The data we possess about the gospel is sufficient to make it sensible for the non-Christian to begin his search for the ultimate clue with Christianity. A display of evidences is aimed at encouraging people to put the gospel to the test and make their decision regarding it. Naturally the evidence we speak about is of a probable kind. Not the surest historical evidence for anything is equivalent to mathematical demonstration. That it is only probable does not mean it is worthless, however. For all legal and historical decisions are made upon the basis of probable judgment based on evidence. Since the whole of life proceeds on such a basis, it is not a weakness that Christian evidences should rest on it too. Human decisions are constantly made on the ground of probable evidence just because they are human. The choice of a world view does not depend on a different principle. The gospel makes a claim, and the claim can be tested by anyone who takes the trouble. Historical pessimism is nice amusement, but not a game anyone can play to the end. The beauty of the gospel consists in its openness to examination. God has revealed himself in time-space history (Jn. 1:14). Christ was a public figure, and his resurrection a public event. The New Testament knows nothing of trans, supra, or meta-history! God acted in history, and it is in history that we seek him.

VIII

THE INADEQUACY OF EXPERIENCE ALONE

The appeal to a personal experience of grace has always been a mark of evangelical Christianity. The gospel throws a direct tangent over to life itself. "The kingdom of God is righteousness, peace and joy, in the Holy Spirit" (Rom. 14:17; 15:13). Apart from an inner testimony of the Spirit, the outward witness to Christ remains a dead letter. However, ours is a day when the witness of the Spirit is radically distorted, changed into an escape from the essential historical and dogmatic *content* of the gospel. Perverted in this way, the appeal to subjective validation can completely blunt the cutting edge of Christian apologetics. In an era preoccupied with man's feeling states, the Christian needs to be watchful that the objectivity of God's acts and words is preserved intact.

Experience alone is too flimsy a base on which to rest the Christian system. The mere fact that a psychological event has taken place in one's brain cannot establish the truthfulness of the gospel or the metaphysical assertions of the biblical world view. Religious sensation by itself can only prove itself. The assertion "God exists" simply does not follow from the assertion "I had an experience of God." A psychological datum cannot automatically lead to a metaphysical discovery. However unique an experience may be, it is capable of a number of radically differing interpretations. It may be only an encounter with one's own subconscious. Those who place all their emphasis on a subjective validating process for apologetics eventually reduce the content of revelation and fit it to their taste. The central thing becomes that which comes across to *me*, rather than what *God* has done and spoken. The reason some theologians favor the use of drugs to heighten religious perception is patent. Whenever the existential cart is put before the historical horse, theology becomes a synthesis of human superstitions, and putting LSD into the communion wine is fair play!

46

An exclusive appeal to experience satisfies the humanistic tenor of our day in its focus on man rather than God. The subject who has faith, rather than an object of faith, receives the attention. When the religious consciousness takes the center of the stage, doctrines recede into the background. Biblical teachings on justification, wrath, atonement, sin, trinity, eschatology, are taken with a grain of salt. For they are only, it is said, experience-qualified concepts, arising from a particular culture, and not essential to the Christian "faith." Israel encountered the nameless Other, the Holy, and called it Yahweh. Other cultures called it Marduk or Zeus. The unity of all religions is found in the numinous awe felt in the presence of the Other. Man's changing conceptions about the nature of the Other are plastic to his time and age. He names the unknown God in the terms he knows. This way of thinking is totally alien to Christianity. In his diverse religions man is *not* seeking after God (Rom. 3:11). The pagan worshiping his idol is not justified by the sincerity of his "faith." Faith in itself is impotent unless it grasps the saving name of Jesus. The attempt to establish religious truth by an appeal to the data of comparative religious experience has proved a failure. Subjective responses alone cannot yield a gospel. The uniqueness of the Christian message is not found at the point of experience at all, but in the incarnation datum.

Unfortunately the evangelical Christian is more vulnerable to the new liberalism than he was to the old. The older variety was more candid in admitting its antisupernaturalism and antipathy to dogma. But the new liberalism is ingeniously subtle. It makes its appeal at the precise point where evangelicals had been placing stress, namely, personal experience. The difference is, however, that personal experience now means the relativity of any known theological and historical content to the gospel. The new liberalism is compatible with any set of circumstances. Faith's "objectivity" turns out to be "subjectivity." God's act is not visible, not testable, not examinable, save through "faith." Instead of receiving valid data and making a decision on that basis, "faith" has been made into a cognitive magic wand, which provides an "object" whenever man exercises the faith function. No doubt these upper-story theologians wish to defend the faith against destructive criticisms; but what an enormous price to pay for that!

Under the new liberal construction it matters little whether the biblical statements are valid propositions for the Church, or whether the biblical events are truly events at all. The only important thing is the experience which the *telling* of these tales induces in the receptive heart. You *can* believe the events are literal and the words true if you like, we are paternally told, but you are not bound to. The only act of God which vitally concerns *me* is the contemporary psychological event, not the far distant historical one. Now this makes apologetics all very easy of course. In the old days a Christian felt bound to refute the charges of the sceptic and cynic. With the new approach it hardly matters if the critic is right. Indeed if faith be a leap, it might even increase our faith if we thought he were! And when we explain that the gospel is only true if you believe it, and on no other grounds, he will walk away smiling, for that is exactly what he thought all the time. A nasty argument has been avoided. A dialogue has taken place. Both receive prizes. Unfortunately one thing is lacking. The lost man has not been told of his need to be saved from wrath through the blood of the Lamb. An appeal to experience is *not* evangelism. Justification does not come at a certain degree of existential temperature. It is a legal declaration about the status of a man properly related to the Savior, *whatever* he may feel like. An experience may be psychological, physiological, theological, or demonic. The existential infection in modern theology has come at a disastrous time. It links hands with the secular flight from reason, and surrenders the very thing which makes Christianity strong, the veracity of God's act into history and the reliability of God's Word in Scripture.

The new theologians seek to draw fire away from their Achilles heel by imputing unworthy motives underlying the desire for objective evidences. The attempt to construct an intelligent faith is made out to be a carnal longing for earthly security. "The greater the doubt, the greater the faith" is the incredible slogan of the new liberals. If you only had "faith," they say, then you would stop clinging to objectivity. True sanctity is the surrendering of Bible and resurrection, and resting only in "God." While this manner of argument is excellent irrationalism, it is bad theology. Faith is a resting of the heart in the sufficiency of the evidences. The modern understanding of faith makes it virtually epistemological suicide. There is nothing to distinguish it from the crassest credulity and gullibility. Religious experiences not subject to testing procedures are used to "prove" everything from Zen to Mormonism. Historical pessimism in the roots of the gospel has nothing to do with faith. On the contrary, doubt in the reality of God's act and word is a mark of *apistia*. Faith is not believing what you know to be absurd. It is trusting what on excellent testimony appears to be true. Luther has been compared favorably with the new liberals in a way that does neither justice to him nor credit to his modern interpreters. Luther abandoned all confidence in his works-righteousness and placed his trust in the finished work of Jesus Christ for salvation. But the new theologian abandons confidence in the intellectual and historical content of the Christian message and places his trust in a subjective man-centered experience which is indistinguishable from gastric upset. There is simply no parallel there. Luther trusted an objectively true gospel, and the new liberals trust a subjectively pleasing state of mind. Luther held to faith in Christ, the new liberal to faith in faith.

Nowhere in the Bible is faith depicted as an unmotivated leap in the dark. Abraham, the father of all who believe, acted upon specific divine promises (Gen. 12:3; 15:5f; Rom. 4:20f; Heb. 11:8-12). Abraham was prepared to act into the future on the *basis* of promises he was confident were divine in their origin. The Christian is expected to view the future with hope because God raised Christ from the dead, that is, to project a present well-founded certainty into the future. Hebrews eleven mentions Gideon as a man of faith too (11:32). But Gideon asked for a notable objective proof of God's word to him (Jdg. 6). Are we to believe that Abraham's faith was one of a different order than Gideon's? In the brief narrative of Genesis we are not told the grounds on which Abraham's certainty rested, but neither does it tell us that these grounds were lacking.

The dramatic conversion of the Apostle Paul is often made a model of the autonomy of faith in isolation from objectifying elements. But the New Testament prevents us from accepting such an inference. Paul's conversion was a miracle designed to authenticate Paul's credentials among the Lord's apostles. It included an audible voice which all the company with him heard (Acts 9:7) and a visible light which everyone saw (22:9). A special vision to Ananias (9:10) concerning his role in the event served to give the whole experience a very objective cast indeed. No doubt some new liberal would

49

wish to object that the light, the sound, and the vision are all Luke's objectifying elements placed in the narrative to improve its dramatic effect for the reader, and that the "real conversion" was inward and personal only. Such argumentation is illicit because it adopts a certain view of Paul's conversion *a priori* and then eliminates all the evidence in the records which contradicts it! Hardly an example of impartial historiography. But Paul did not rest satisfied with these proofs. Immediately he began searching out proofs from the Old Testament that Jesus was indeed the Messiah promised (Acts 9:22; 17:2f; 28:23). Later he visited the Jerusalem apostles, not to talk about the weather, but to gather further information, historical and doctrinal, essential to the gospel (Gal. 1:18; I Cor. 15:3-11). The art of dangling the gospel on a subjective skyhook, while minimizing its historical grounding, is a very recent skill, and one in which a serious Christian witness hardly need develop proficiency.

The bitter fruit of this trend toward *faith in faith* is the irrelevance of all history and truth. Empty tomb, ransom, hell, judgment, infallibility, Jonah, virgin birth—all can be safely jettisoned as nonessential baggage which have little to do with religious experience. Gospel truth can just be revised to suit the consensus of the community (whatever community is suited to your taste). This whole mentality is a million miles distant from the New Testament message. It is a hermeneutic (a way of interpretation) which compares existential temperatures and ignores what Christ and the apostles *taught*. The first disciples pointed away from their experiences to the evidences that a divine Savior had entered history, a fact amply attested by the bodily resurrection. This Lord and Savior had instructed his disciples on the meaning of his impending death (Mk. 10:45) and directed them to a deposit of God's written Word found in sacred Scripture (Lk. 24:45). This claim can be enquired into and examined for its credibility, and when considered, can yield positive results.

Whereas scepticism is marked by bleak despair, the gospel of Christ yields richest joy. Experience does play an important, even indispensable role in personal verification. But it cannot stand alone apart from other considerations. Redemption has been accomplished by the Lamb of God; now it needs to be appropriated. Men will put their trust in Christ only when we preach him in the power of the Spirit. Our part is to present Christ as intelligently and fervently as we can, and wait for the breath of heaven. Paul warns us against a false emphasis. He says in effect: "Do not crow about spiritual resurrections, and do not boast in religious experiences, *unless* Christ has actually been raised in time-space history!" (I Cor. 15:14, an expanded paraphrase). The gospel yields deep joy, and not the least of the reasons it does so is that it is *true*.

IX

THE HISTORICAL DOCUMENTS

Since the death of the first generation of Christians, no one has been able to interview firsthand the eyewitnesses of Christ's life, death, and resurrection. We are dependent upon written human testimony of the kind utilized in all historical study. But this is no cause for despair because the documents we possess are of the highest possible calibre. Pessimism concerning the trustworthiness of the New Testament is utterly unwarranted, and generally reflects ignorance of the facts. It is a matter of public *fact*, not of unreflecting *faith*, that the historical foundations underneath the Christian message are exceedingly secure.

While it is true that the original manuscripts of the four Gospels have not survived, we do possess literally thousands of copies in codices and papyrus fragments, and attestation in the writings of the earliest Fathers. In order to demonstrate that this state of affairs is by no means an inherent weakness in validating the gospel, it is fitting to produce a set of comparisons from the area of ancient documents. The Roman historian Tacitus, writing early in the second century concerning events half a century earlier, is considered a first rate historical source for the period *despite* the fact that the oldest manuscript copy of his work which remains dates from a full millennium after he wrote, and that we possess only twenty good manuscripts in all! In like manner a full thousand years separates the writings of Caesar's *Gallic Wars* and the date of the oldest manuscript we now have. Aristotle wrote his *Poetics* three and a half centuries B.C. and the oldest manuscript dates from the eleventh century A.D., a full fourteen hundred years later! The same is true of the Greek historian Thucydides of whose work the oldest manuscript was copied thirteen hundred years after his death. In every single case cited, critical scholars do not think of dismissing the evidence because the original manuscripts have not survived. Each of the writers is considered an A-1 historical source.

In the case of the New Testament, however, the textual witness is remarkably superior. No less than four thousand Greek manuscripts have survived; and one of the best, Vaticanus, dates from a mere three hundred years after the composition of the Gospels. The Chester Beatty papyri containing extensive portions of the New Testament date back to A.D. 150, while the Rylands fragment of John comes from A.D. 120. In addition we have attestation of the text in the Apostolic fathers from the turn of the first century. In short, on objective grounds, we have before us documents of the greatest possible value for ascertaining the facts about Jesus Christ. The widespread distrust of the Gospels does not stem from any knowledge of the facts but from anti-Christian propaganda.

Moreover, it is possible to estimate with a fair degree of certainty exactly when each of the Gospels was actually written. The Gospel of Mark must have been composed in its final draft about three decades after the resurrection. Early tradition consistently connects it to the apostle Peter who was martyred in the mid-sixties of the first century, and there is nothing in the Gospel which gives any hint of knowledge about the catastrophe which befell Palestine in A.D. 70. The Gospel of Matthew which incorporates Markan material was written soon after. The special Matthean sections in the Gospel reflect a strongly Jewish interest which connects the author and his sources with the earliest Church. Very likely the Gospel of Luke was written earlier still, prior to the death of Peter and Paul, about A.D. 62. The legal details in the trial narrative of the Gospel and the geographical and cultural accuracy of Acts, also written by Luke, call for an early date and presuppose close research on the part of the writer. The fact that Acts does not record the death of Paul is compelling reason to suppose this had not occurred at the time of writing. Tradition places John's Gospel in the last decade of the first century. But its Jewish character and topographical accuracy imply that its author or his sources come from Palestine before the fall of Jerusalem in A.D. 70. Recent criticism of John has reversed completely the older scepticism, and come out strongly in favor of its substantial accuracy.

We possess then four outstanding documents written within a few decades of the resurrection and incorporating sources that go back much further. And all these documents claim directly or indirectly an eyewitness basis for the events they record.

There has been, however, a concerted attempt recently to get behind the written Gospels and undermine their integrity from another angle. Radical "form criticism" of the Gospels is the theory that the documents were not written out of an accurate historical memory, but concocted out of the creative imagination of the Christian community. By accepting "form criticism" as a legitimate literary form in Scripture, Catholic and Protestant scholars alike have joined hand with sceptics of the past to allege myth, invention, and fraud in the very heart of our New Testament records. This fact is grievous, not because the allegations have any firm basis in reality, but because it reveals a profound theological sickness in all the churches today. The form critical hypothesis is untenable because of a lack of any positive evidence for it. If the Gospels were composed to deal with the problems of the post-resurrection churches, the editing boards were singularly inept. Where in the four Gospels does one find the problem of tongues discussed, or the admission of the Gentiles, or the government of the churches? Not one single problem we *know* about in the apostolic church is raised in the Gospels directly. Every form-critical verdict is based on a circular argument. It is *assumed* that the Gospels are sources for the history of the early church, and then it proceeds to exegete them accordingly. But, until one piece of positive evidence turns up to explain *how* the community, scattered around the then known world, conspired together to perform so gigantic a fraud in the space of three decades, form criticism is unproven speculation. If our concern is for facts, we shall have to admit that if something has been "dissolved" in the current discussion it is form criticism itself rather than the figure of Jesus Christ.

As opposed to the biblical emphasis on history, rationalism has always tended to be antihistorical. Historical knowledge was felt to be second-rate knowledge because the degree of certainty in it was so far less than mathematical. While this mood did produce its own historians, the positivists, who sought to find this certainty in history, more often than not it produced a disengagement from history. Theologians sought to rescue the Christian faith from the fear of falsification through historical criticism by shutting it up in the subjective realm. This is the strategy adopted by Barth, Brunner,

54

Bultmann, Tillich, Bornkamm, and a host of others. But it is utterly opposed by the New Testament insistence that God decisively revealed himself in the empirical realm through Jesus Christ, in the midst of ordinary secular history, in the flesh and bone of history itself. The separation of saving history from ordinary history is monstrous. There is only one history. And the gospel claims that God showed himself in that. When we ground our apologetic in historical data, we are merely doing what the apostles did before us. If the gospel cannot be sustained by historical data, it cannot be sustained at all. Faith rests upon the certainty of what God did in history (Lk. 1:1-4). The current historical heresy espoused by Dilthey and Collingwood, that there can be no objective knowledge of the past, has been swallowed by a raft of Christian apologists. The result of losing contact with the historic Christ is always the same, the "contemporary Christ" created in the image of his human maker. This dogma about history is false, and directly antithetical to the Christian faith. The fact is that we can come to know Jesus Christ historically before we know him personally. Indeed we *must*. Otherwise the Christ we know personally is the mirror of our own visage.

Indeed all the evidence is against form-critical hypothesis. Paul was careful to keep a distinction between his words and those of his Lord (I Cor. 7:12). Parables abound in the Gospels and are virtually absent from the epistles. Apostlic eyewitnesses governed the Church, exercising a control over any mythmaking tendencies. The Son of Man title is used by Jesus himself in the gospels, and is not used of him in the epistles. This proves that a clear boundary was respected between the gospels as historical records and the epistles as church doctrine. The aim of all the gospels is given by Luke (1:1-4):

> Inasmuch as many have undertaken to compile a narrative of the things which have been accomplished among us, *just as* they were delivered to us by those who from the beginning were *eye-witnesses* and ministers of the word, it seemed good to me also, having followed all things closely for some time past, to write an *orderly account* for you, most excellent Theophilus, that you may know the *truth* [certainty] concerning the things of which you may have been informed.

The Jewish procedure of handing down historical materials was not a haphazard and unorganized accident. The oral tradition was checked by written records, and the written documents were handled with scrupulous care. This fastidious care is demonstrated in the transmission of the Hebrew text of the Old Testament. A comparison of the Isaiah scroll from the Qumram library with the Isaiah of the Massoretic text has proved that only the tiniest variations occurred during a full thousand years of copying! It is entirely possible that Matthew was added to the band of the disciples because of his training in scribal techniques and kept written notes of the teachings and activities of Jesus. At any rate there is no basis for suspecting that the figure of Jesus was a figment of a communal imagination. Such criticism would reduce every historical figure to a puff of wind. All that we ask, is for a person to keep his antisupernatural bias isolated from his historical integrity if only for the time it takes to face the person of Jesus Christ fairly. If we apply the same historical standards to the Gospels which we apply to Tacitus and Aristotle, our validation of the Christian message is well on the way.

It is often asked in this connection how much extra-Biblical corroboration of the Gospels we possess. Often the notion behind this is the belief that the Christian writers are to be held suspect until cleared by non-Christian sources (presumably unbiased). The notion is utterly fallacious, and reverses normal historical procedure. *All* data pertaining to a given question deserves a hearing, and deserves to stand on its own merits. Even if there were not a single piece of extra-Biblical attestation, a person would still be confronted with superb historical sources. There is, however, a body of testimonies in Jewish and Gentile writing which touch on the Biblical history. The Talmud contains some hostile but historically valuable allusions to the life of Jesus. His followers believed him virgin born, he performed miracles, and was executed for heresy. The Jewish historian Josephus fills in many details concerning the rulers mentioned in the New Testament (the Herods, Pilate, Festus, Agrippa), and alluded to the claims of Jesus and the belief in his resurrection. Of the early Gentile writers, Thallus records a solar eclipse during the crucifixion of Christ, but generally the pagan writers had no interest in what they considered to be a vulgar oriental cult. The place to look would be the police records of the Roman Empire if these had survived! Tacitus refers to the great fire of Rome which Nero blamed on the Christians and mentions Christ's execution under Pontius Pilate.

The Gospels were written by brave men, many of whom were

called upon to die for their historical claims. There was nothing to gain by forgery or deceit. Their works were written in association with eyewitnesses of the events they record, and enjoy a rich textual witness second to none. The gospel message could scarcely possess a sounder historical base by any standard.

X

THE FACT OF CHRIST

There exists no document from the ancient world witnessed by so excellent a set of textual and historical testimonies, and offering so superb an array of historical data on which an intelligent decision may be made. An honest man cannot dismiss a source of this kind. Scepticism regarding the historical credentials of Christianity is based upon an irrational bias.

Christianity is Christ. It is only appropriate to begin with him when investigating the claims of the Christian gospel. He is the center both of our theology and apologetics. In addition, he is almost universally admired and respected for his wisdom, his character, and his beneficial effect upon the world. An intelligent non-Christian owes it to himself to conduct an investigation into the roots of the Christian message if only to be sure his unbelief is not itself an unfounded prejudice.

Once we open the gospels and encounter Jesus, we are impressed at the enormous difference between the popular concept of Christ and the figure actually portrayed on their pages. Whereas the Christ of modern mythology is a mild-mannered humanist, standing for vague ideals and turning the other cheek to his enemies, the Christ of the New Testament is an intrepid egoist. In every Gospel, in almost every chapter, he is found making amazing claims for himself, which are most shocking if they are not true. He claimed authority over all venerable tradition, he forgave man's sins, he controlled natural forces, he boldly predicted his own resurrection and coming again to judge the world. Eventually the authorities had enough of it and put him to death for blasphemy. Jesus was not unwilling to die, for he saw death as part of his redeeming mission, but he reiterated time and again that death would not hold him, and that his resurrection would decisively prove his claims. The ultimate test of his truthfulness lay in a future miracle.

Before developing the nature and importance of Christ's claims, it is necessary to discuss the so-called "quest for the historical Jesus" and the reason for its failure. This quest was the attempt to reconstruct the historical Jesus as he really was. It was often an attempt to delve behind the Christ of myth and dogma, and rediscover the purely human Jesus of Nazareth. The quest ended in hopeless failure, but the reason it did is seldom grasped. It is common to hold that the quest failed because the historical sources for the quest are inappropriate for an inductive scientific investigation, or because the Christ of faith cannot be approached objectively at all. Neither of these reasons is true, however. The Gospel accounts are superb historical records on any reckoning and quite capable of yielding positive results. Furthermore, as we have seen already, the essence of the gospel is that the Christ of faith is precisely the Jesus of history and none other. The uniqueness of the Christian message is its open-to-investigation form. The actual reason for failure lies elsewhere. The Jesus of history eluded the historians, not because the sources were "kerygmatic" nor because the incarnation took place in "supra-history," but for the simple reason that a purely human Jesus like they sought never existed! The nineteenth century liberals had decided well in advance of their quest that the only Jesus they were prepared to discover was a naturalistic one. The error in the old quest was not its inductive methodology (that was its virtue), but rather its antisupernatural bias. Of course Jesus eluded their quest since every piece of data we possess presents a divine Messiah. Imagine a quest for the historical Napoleon based on the presumption that every source about his life lied in its fundamental understanding! Such historical pessimism makes the whole science of historiography a ridiculous farce. Seeing correctly the true fallacy of the old quest also gives us the reason why the new quest will fail too. All the new quest has really done is to retain what it ought to have rejected (the naturalistic bias) and rejected what it ought to have retained (the inductive procedure). Its future is not bright. Soon the break with any subject-object distinction will be complete, and the past will entirely vanish. And when the knowledge of the past disappears, men will be condemned to repeat every foolish heresy and error they made before.

But for those uninterested in theological games, and wanting to examine the actual data history bequeaths us, the historical Jesus is not a problem at all. He is less of a problem than Julius Caesar or Alexander the Great. The Christ of the New Testament is readily approachable and rather easier to understand than we would sometimes wish. It is important to begin with Jesus Christ, because it involves no dogmatic preconceptions. Anyone can conduct the simple investigation. However irritating it may be to non-Christian and existentialist theologian alike, *whosoever will* may come to Jesus, ask him intelligent questions, and put their trust in him. Christian evidences merely press the evangelical invitation home to consider *him*. It was a consideration of the historical facts regarding Jesus Christ that prepared C. S. Lewis to take the gospel seriously. All the evidence of the New Testament points in the same direction—to a Messiah who is both human and divine, and to whom men owe all their allegiance. It matters not whether we read Matthew, Mark, Luke, or John, Peter, Paul, James, or Jude, the message is the same. The only understanding of Christ which is *not* based upon a speculative reconstruction of the historical materials is one of worship and praise, "My Lord and my God!" The divine Christ is the only Christ of which any document in the New Testament has any knowledge.

"What do you think of the Christ? Whose son is he?" is the question Jesus posed to the people of his day (Mt. 22:42). His amazing claims both in words and in action constantly confronted onlookers with the Christological question. When he rode into Jerusalem on a donkey to fulfill the ancient prophecy (Zc. 9:9), all the city was stirred to ask, "Who is this?" (Mt. 21:10). After Jesus had offered a pardon to the paralytic for his sins, the enemies of Jesus became deeply troubled as they faced the unpalatable alternatives—either he was a dangerous charlatan, or else a divine Messiah (Lk. 5:21). The question of Christ's true identity is the most basic in the gospel. Jesus makes a decision inescapable. The whole texture of the Gospels is riddled with egocentric teachings. He believed the whole prophetic Scripture was focused on his person (Lk. 4:16). The Kingdom of God was drawing nigh because he was in the midst of men (Mk. 1:15; Lk. 17:21). Nothing short of total discipleship was demanded of his followers (Mk. 8:34). Otherwise men were not worthy of him (Mt. 10:38). His teachings rang with the great *I AM* statements which are divine claims in structure and content (Exod. 3:14; Jn. 4:26; 6:35; 8:12; 10:9; 11:25). When one considers that all these claims came from the lips of the humblest of men, his breath is taken away with amazement. Clearly Jesus made direct claims for himself and his importance. One title he liked to use of himself was "son of man." It is drawn from the apocalyptic passage in Daniel (7:13f) in which the divine figure appears before God, and receives a universal kingdom and everlasting dominion. At his trial Jesus forced a decision by deliberately identifying this figure with himself (Mk. 14:62). His coming to earth, however, was structured in two stages: first as the Servant of the Lord (Isa. 53) to render sacrifice and satisfaction for the sins of many (Mk. 10:45), and second, as the Son of Man (Dan. 7) to receive the glory and honor due him and to reign over men (Mt. 16:27; 19:28). At this present time, therefore, men are invited to appropriate the finished work of redemption he performed on behalf of sinners, before the day of grace is exhausted and they must face him as their judge (Jn. 5:27).

The claims of Jesus were not all direct ones. His assumption of the right to pronounce forgiveness shocked the onlookers (Mk. 2:7). Only a miracle could balance the situation (2:9-12). Impressive was the authority with which he taught (Mt. 7:28f) and the claim that his words had eternal validity (Mt. 24:35; Jn. 12:48). Every one of his miracles had the force of a dramatized claim: healing the sick, casting out demons, stilling the water, multiplying the loaves, restoring sight, raising the dead. The significance of these acts was not lost upon those who witnessed and heard of them. This was an extraordinary divine Person who had to be reckoned with. The destinies of all men were suspended on their relationship with him.

The person who will consider the claims of Christ seriously cannot avoid making a decision on the basis of them. The possible alternatives are not numerous either. Jesus does not give us much room to move in. These are shocking alternatives. C. S. Lewis put it this way:

> A Man who was merely a man and said the sort of things Jesus said would not be a great moral teacher. He would either be a lunatic—on a level with the man who says he is a poached egg—or else he would be the Devil of Hell. You must make your choice. Either this man was, and is, the Son of God: or else a madman or something worse. You can shut him up for

a fool, you can spit at Him and kill Him as a demon; or you can fall at His feet and call Him Lord and God. But let us not come with any patronising nonsense about His being a great human teacher. He has not left that open to us. He did not intend to (*Mere Christianity*, Fontana, 1952, 52f).

Lewis is right. Either a fraud has taken place at some stage, or else Jesus is the divine Son of God. The non-Christian cannot avoid claiming a fraud if he would evade Jesus. But proving it is quite another matter. The theory that Jesus himself perpetrated this fraud, that he was a deceiver, a charlatan, a liar, a scoundrel, has never appealed to people. It is so transparently ridiculous. The high level of his ethical and religious teaching makes any such theory utterly untenable. It is perhaps possible that he performed this fraud innocently. Was he deluded about his greatness, a paranoid, an unintentional deceiver, a schizophrenic? Again the skill and depth of his teachings support the case only for his total mental soundness. If only we were as sane as he! No theory that Jesus Christ himself engineered a deception can stand the test of even a superficial examination. Is it conceivable then that the fraud entered in the years after his death, when his followers began to trump up his importance because they loved him? This theory suffers from a similar objection. The apostles were simple fishermen, unsophisticated and honest men. Their record of sincerety and teaching does not approve the theory of deception either. They would hardly have been prepared to die for something they themselves had cooked up most deceitfully. Besides, the Messiah they allegedly invented was most unlike any Messiah most people were looking for, and they got the same hostile treatment as their Lord himself did. Far from wanting to deify him, his Jewish disciples themselves found that fact hard to accept and did so only under the strongest divine pressures. The people of that day wanted a kingly Messiah, not a suffering Servant; they wanted a human political deliverer, not a divine spiritual Savior.

The dilemma of Christ's identity will not be easily side-stepped. The most sensible solution is to bow to the force of the evidence for his divinity. Jesus is either guilty of criminal megalomania, or actually the person he claims to be. Once a non-Christian has faced the issue this way he will not be easily able to shake off his responsibility to decide the issue once and for all.

XI

ON THE THIRD DAY

The central motif in the preaching of the earliest disciples was the resurrection of Jesus Christ from death. To them it was the decisive proof that the gospel was true. Here was an event in the stream of world history which boldly demonstrated the existence of God and his intentions for the salvation of men. The fact of the resurrection is an undigestible surd for the naturalist. Yet the birth of the Church cannot be explained without this event. It is a focus for both theology and apologetics, because it enters into both God's redemptive provision (Rom. 4:25) and the ground of certainty (I Pt. 1:3). In addition to laying redemptive groundwork for deliverance, Christ came to demonstrate that the "unknown God" is no longer unknown (Acts 17:23,31). The resurrection is a fact of history without which history does not make sense. God has acted in the empirical realm, in the flesh and bone of history, in order to save men from both sin and agnosticism. All of the false Messiahs have vanished from history. The only explanation for the existence of the gospel is the bodily resurrection of the Lord.

In considering the fact of the resurrection we come into content with genuine historical materials. Again we are not interested in *demonstration*, for historical decisions are not capable of such proof. But we are not on that account pessimistic about the value of the evidence. A lawyer, Frank Morrison set out to write a book disproving the resurrection claim of the Christian Church, but the stubbornness of the facts prevented the book from being written. He started out with a bias against the resurrection, but was compelled by honesty to revise his presuppositions. While it is true that historical facticity is not the *only* facet of the resurrection which is important, it is also true that the resurrection is nothing without it. And furthermore, to the non-Christian, factuality is the decisive question, for upon it hangs his decision whether to entrust his life to Christ or not, for time and eternity. The resurrection has tremendous significance for Christian apologetics. It had the same importance for Jesus too. For he literally staked his entire reputation as a teacher of truth upon the prediction that he would rise from the grave (Lk. 17:31-33). The integrity of both gospel and Savior rests upon the validity of this single event.

The validity of the Christian claim turns very much upon the fact of the resurrection on the third day. While recent theological writing contains abundant references to the event, very little in the way of evidence is offered for this crucial datum. Many have sought to hold the Easter faith entirely apart from historical reasoning, and even against it. Knowledge of the resurrection is supposed to come by revelation, not by historical study. In that case it is difficult to understand, first, why the apostles pointed to an event at all, and second, why their testimony matters if the resurrection be "immediately" known. If the *effects* of the resurrection be known, as they are, there is nothing that can stop extrapolating back from the effect to the cause. The motivation behind the attempt to cover over historical evidence is due of course to the "upper story" mentality which afflicts theology today.

It is crucial in evangelism and apologetics to have objective considerations to back up the claims for the gospel. The sinner needs to know that the gospel is not the concoction of a human imagination, but is objectively true. The importance of this can be illustrated in an imaginary conversation.

John makes a claim: "I have a five-leaf clover in my room."

Mary challenges it: "I don't believe you. Let's have a look."

John retorts: "Oh it's there all right, but I can't let you see it."

Mary replies: "Why should I believe you when you refuse an investigation?"

Mary's point is well taken. It *is* absurd to claim an objective five-leaf clover on the one hand, and then refuse to contemplate any procedures of verification. No less absurd is the new theology which claims an objective resurrection and then adds that any historical investigation is out of the question. The person who professes the resurrection but denies all objective evidence for it is kidding nobody but himself. No non-Christian will be impressed with such double-talk. His only conclusion will be that such a believer does not hold

64

the resurrection to be a historical fact, but only an existential experience in his own life.

At the forefront of the historical evidence for the supreme miracle of Christianity stands the empty tomb. A scarce three months after the death of Jesus in Jerusalem, his disciples were found proclaiming his bodily resurrection. Very few of the Jewish or Roman leaders were sympathetic with the new movement which promised to upset the religious balance which had been achieved in Judaea with some difficulty. We may safely presume that, had they been able to, they would have successively disproven the Christian claim and nipped the whole movement in the bud. Yet although the apostles encountered the stiffest opposition to their ministry in Jerusalem, no one was able successfully to falsify their claim that Jesus rose from the grave! The easiest way to have done this would have been to produce the body of Jesus. Neither the Jewish nor the Roman authorities had any motive for keeping it hidden. Apparently it was missing from the tomb in which it had been laid. The Jews invented a story about the disciples stealing the body (Mt. 28:11-15) but this obvious fabrication has never carried much weight. Hypocrites do not become martyrs. The disciples might have been deluded, but they were not liars. Besides there was the practical problem of getting around the guard which Pilate set at the tomb (Mt. 27:65). Grave robbers could have been responsible for removing the body except for the absence of any monetary motive for doing so and the same difficulty of breaking the seal and escaping the guards. One of the most decisive proofs for the resurrection is provided unwillingly by the enemies of Jesus who were clearly frustrated in any attempt they made to disprove the claim that Jesus rose.

Various theories of intentional deception on the part of Jesus or the disciples have been proposed in the past. The old swoon theory was that Jesus never actually died on the cross but survived crucifixion, escaped from the tomb, and presented himself alive to his followers. This theory is harder to believe than the biblical account. It is past belief how Jesus could have survived a crucifixion of six hours and a Roman spear wound, and convinced Pilate and his executioners that he was dead. Then in a state of terrible physical pain he endured the coldness of the tomb for three days, removed the large boulder at the door of the grave, eluded the guard posted at the sepulchre, convinced his disciples that he had a glorious resurrection body, and finally disappeared and died in anonymity. A hypothesis of this sort only emphasizes how far a non-Christian will go to escape the inescapable. H. J. Schonfield has a new twist. This deception was in Jesus' mind when he planned to fake death and conjure up a resurrection. He was to receive a pain killing drug while on the cross to enable him to survive the ordeal. The whole "Passover plot" fell through, however, when the unexpected happened—a Roman soldier thrust his spear in Jesus' side and the conspiracy was foiled. Aside from the intrinsic improbabilities of Jesus' deliberate deception based on his known character, the theory collapses upon the fact of the empty tomb. How did the conspiritors dispose of the body in the end, and convince people the resurrection really happened? The problem remains as big as ever.

Of even greater importance to the disciples in the line of evidences for the resurrection was the series of appearances which the risen Christ made to chosen witnesses (Acts 10:41). Paul gives the earliest list of such appearances (I Cor. 15:5-9). The appearance to Peter is put first. Strictly speaking Christ came first to Mary Magdalene (Jn. 20:11-18), but Paul does not wish to include the name of a female in a list which has almost legal force in his mind. The fact that John does record it is impressive because it is a detail which no first century male would have invented! But John had the courage to record it, and the story has important symbolic overtones (cf. Lk. 8:2; Mt. 27:55f). The appearance to Peter and James individually and separately goes far to explain their unique authority in the primitive Jewish Church. The appearance to five hundred brethren at once indicates the public nature of the evidence. Many of these believers Paul knew to be alive at the time of his writing (I Cor. 15:6). This extensive series of appearances to many individuals over a period of several weeks is a phenomenon which calls for an explanation. Jesus left the clear impression in his disciples that he was neither the ghost of a dead man nor simply a revived corpse. He was alive in a new mode of existence, and he summoned his disciples to proclaim the possibility of such existence for all who will believe on his name. These appearances were either actual and substantial, or else they were hallucinatory. A hallucina-

66

tion is an apparent perception of an object. It appears frequently at the end of a period of anxious wishfulness for something to happen, and to isolated persons, not to groups. It is striking that all of the factors favorable to the hallucination hypothesis are absent from the New Testament. The resurrection caught everyone off guard. The disciples were surprised and disbelieving for joy (Mk. 16:8; Mt. 28:17; Lk. 24:36-43; Jn. 20:19). They needed convincing themselves. Jesus did not come into an atmosphere of wishful thinking. His appearances occurred at unpredictable times and in odd places. No psychological gymnastics accompanied them. They just happened. Many had the experience at the same time too, affording correlation and corroboration. Furthermore, physical aspects to the appearances such as his invitation to Thomas to touch him, and his eating with the disciples, add to the impressiveness of the appearances. The birth and growth of the early church is utterly inexplicable apart from the appearances of the risen Christ. Only the resurrection itself offers an adequate rational explanation to the facts we see.

There is a fantastic difference between the disciples who appear in the Gospel narratives and those who figure in the book of Acts. Timid, unreliable, fearful, unbelieving men emerge from the events immediately following the death of Christ bursting to tell of his resurrection whatever the cost to their own personal safety. Peter had returned to his fishing in Galilee (Jn. 21:1ff), but later crashed onto the Jerusalem scene to announce the resurrection which he had witnessed (Acts 2:32; 3:15). James had formerly been sceptical (Jn. 7:5) but after a resurrection appearance (I Cor. 15:7) took the helm of the mother church in Jerusalem (Acts 15:13; Gal. 1:19). The entire narrative of the Acts of the Apostles is posited upon this single event. It is woven into its very fabric. The disciples were intellectually convinced that the gospel was true, because God had raised Jesus from the dead. The conversion of Paul from his bitter hostility to the Christian movement in the beginning to his energetic defense of the gospel all around the Mediterranean world is further testimony to the resurrection. It was the only appearance Christ made to an avowed enemy of his. "Nothing but a sudden, unexpected, objective, irresistible revelation of the Resurrected One Himself in the majesty of his divine power could convince and convert a man like Saul. It was such an appearance which was given him," wrote D. A. Hayes. Paul's entire ministry thereafter is massive testimony to the reality of Christ's resurrection.

There are very few events of ancient history better attested with sound evidence than the resurrection of Jesus Christ. It is as secure in its place in the annals of history as almost any other event. The resurrection is the only hypothesis which will make peace with all the facts. It constitutes excellent motivation for trusting Christ. Its evidence is sufficiently impressive to demand an answer from every non-Christian. The documentary evidence is superb. Few facts enjoy such corroboration. The resurrection stands within the realm of historical factuality.

XII

SOLA SCRIPTURA

The Christian message is historical to the core. All of its doctrines arise from God's self-disclosure in history. Its doctrine of authority, therefore, is given in the disclosure situations of redemptive history; that is, the nature of Scripture is determined from the teachings of divinely authenticated messengers, Jesus Christ and his apostles. The entire edifice of theology is built upon this epistemological foundation. Without the propositional revelation in Scripture, theology is an impossible endeavor; and yet acceptance of biblical authority is not an unfounded assumption. The work of the theologian does not hang from a sky hook. The resurrection of Jesus Christ establishes his truthfulness in all things. The evangelical doctrine of authority is grounded in the God-given teachings (Jn. 7:16) of the risen Lord himself. His view of Scripture must be the view of his disciples. The Bible is not infallible because *it* says so—but because *he* says so. There is no more reliable witness to the nature of Scripture than the one who died and rose to be our Savior. According to Jesus, divine revelation is mediated in a written record with the authority of God speaking. What the Scripture says, God says (Mt. 5:18; 19:4; Jn. 10:34; Acts 4:25; 28:25; Heb. 10:15). Whether or not we receive the testimony to Scripture as an infallible record of God's revelation is a commentary on the consistency of our Christian discipleship. It is not difficult to understand a biblical critic doubting the veracity of the Scripture who cares nothing for its divine Savior, but it is strange to find a believer professing his Lord and then disregarding Christ's doctrine of inspiration. The authority of Scripture rests upon the datum of the incarnation. As soon as a person comes to faith in the divine Son of God, the question of authority is settled.

Until relatively recent times, Christians have seen the logic of this pattern of authority. The Lord rules his Church by the Word and Spirit. Scripture was the ground for believing revealed truths. Now all of that has changed. A destructive principle has been admitted, the *dichotomy* of biblical errancy. If something is taught in Scripture, it may *or* may not be true. In other words, Scripture is not the ground for believing anything. If the Bible errs in minor matters, perhaps it errs also in major ones; if in incidental things, perhaps in substantial things as well. In the past, the battle lines were fairly closely drawn between the sceptics on the one hand who charged errors and defects in Scripture, and believers on the other hand who stoutly resisted such allegations. Now the average biblical critic who is a member of a Christian church is glad to admit the sceptic's charges and puts up little resistance to his assaults. The reason for this about face is the disengagement from history noted in chapter two. The new theologian is so afraid of uncertainty in historical research that he immunizes his gospel from all contact with the "facts." His kerygma is capable only of subjective validation and neither errors in biblical history nor fallacies in biblical doctrine bother him any more. But they *ought* to bother him! The credibility of the Christian message is bound up with the reliability of its historical proclamation. The very integrity of Jesus Christ rests on the truths of his doctrine of authority. There is no real alternative to the dilemma, either a divine Savior and an infallible Bible, or a fallible Bible and no divine Savior. From the documents alone it is possible to learn that they are reliable to a substantial degree (see chapter nine), but from Jesus Christ we learn their divinely inspired nature. Their general reliability is a matter of public fact; their infallibility is a doctrine revealed through Jesus Christ.

For many today, however, the question of what Jesus Christ taught about Scripture cannot be seriously faced because the evidence against biblical infallibility is so overwhelming that it is hardly relevant. Negative biblical criticism has conducted a wide campaign of brainwashing to this effect. Irresponsible spokesmen contend that no intelligent person could hold to a concept of verbal inspiration. It would require intellectual suicide to believe in biblical inerrancy. It is a silly idolatry and an absurd rationality, they say. All this talk is very intimidating to the young Christian until he stumbles upon one piece of unadmitted information. The "errors" of the Bible are a very slippery lot. Just when you have your hands on one, it evades you and disappears. At bottom these "errors" are really only *difficulties masquerading as errors*. In 1800 the French Institute in Paris issued a list of 82 errors in the Bible which they believed would destroy Christianity. Today none of these "errors" remain! With further reflection and new discoveries, these "errors" were cleared away. Surely it will be so with all such difficulties. We have our Savior's word for that. Criticism has unquestionably made some advances in the understanding of Scripture. But in its speculative theories in the field of higher criticism, there have been many reversals. The real question is: When does a difficulty become an error? The critics claimed a host of "errors" in 1850 which were recanted by 1950. The existence of the Hittites who were an "error" in 1900 are not even a problem today due to archeological finds. It is imperative to distinguish between a difficulty not-yet-solved and an "error." Errors are inconsistent with an infallible Bible, but difficulties are *not*. A little humility on the part of the critic, and a little more corroboration on the part of the archeologist and linguist may change the picture entirely. The evangelical Christian is well aware that unsolved difficulties exist in the biblical text, but he is unwilling for that reason alone to make a rash verdict about biblical infallibility. His doctrine of Scripture, like all his beliefs, derive not from his independent research, but from the doctrine of Scripture his Lord has advanced. Belief in biblical infallibility ought not to be jettisoned because difficulties are known to exist in the text. On the authority of Jesus Christ we have the assurance that these "errors" are far more apparent than real.

Confidence in the happy outcome of biblical research is not blind trust. The number of significant reversals in biblical criticism in the past one hundred years has been extensive. A century ago the book of Genesis was considered a hopeless collection of unsubstantiated myths. Moses, it was thought, would have been unable to write. The Hittites had never existed. The literature was put together with scissors and paste at the hands of fairly unintelligent ancient bookmakers. Then the avalanche of discovery in the Near East came to bury these preposterous theories. Egyptian and Hittite parallels turned up in abundance. Personal names and customs were found echoed in the Amarna letters, the Nuzi tablets, and the Ugaritic texts. The fanciful criteria for discerning literary strands in the documents of the Pentateuch have been subjected to severe criticism, and abandoned by many. Writing in the Near East was already a well-established art in the second millennium B.C. If critics continue to point to Genesis with allegations of "error" they will do so despite the evidence, not because of it.

The book of Deuteronomy provides another striking example. For some years a sixth century date for the book of Deuteronomy has been regarded as an assured result of criticism. It was alleged to be the book read aloud to King Josiah in connection with his reform of religion. On such a view, the book, which depicts the later life and teachings of Moses, is fraudulent. The recent discovery of historical data, however has emphasized the antiquity and authenticity of Deuteronomy. Its entire historical and theological stance is manifestly pre-monarchy. But the discovery of the Hittite covenant codes at Hattusa and other vassal treaties from Assyrian and Aramaic sources has contributed factual evidence for a radical reversal. For the similarity of these treaties to the literary structure of Deuteronomy is striking: preamble, historical prologue, stipulations, sanctions, dynastic disposition. The comparison indeed compels us to recognize that the origin of Deuteronomy *as a unit* lies in the second millennium, not in the first. The facts are opposed to the modern critical theory, and demand a reconsideration.

The book of Daniel too has suffered much in the critics' den. It has been taken for a thinly disguised forgery purporting to describe the events of the fifth century B.C. while actually reflecting on the events of the second. Historical blunders and linguistic anachronisms were referred to as proof of pseudepigraphy. The facts, however, point in a different direction. The discovery of the Elephantine papyri make it difficult to lay much stress on the Aramaic of Daniel, and our knowledge of the early contacts between the Greek and Palestinian civilization naturally explains the presence of Greek loanwords in the text of Daniel. Better knowledge of the neo-Babylonian and Persian periods has largely cleared up the historical problems. The fresh evidence backing a strong view of biblical authenticity ought to encourage the believer under heavy pressure from critical propaganda. Other Old Testament examples of reversals could be cited easily. Suffice it to say criticism is in great flux, and "errors" in the Bible cannot be easily charged. Biblical critics have often been hasty in their scepticism and uncontrolled in their speculations. If they are not prepared to revise their theories in the light of the new evidence, then it is they, and not the so-called "conservatives," who have their heads in the sand.

There are several notable examples of critical reversals in the New Testament too. One example is the book of Acts. In the last century the work was considered by many to be a second century fabrication of the history of the first, a romance designed to cover up the Petro-Pauline rift in the primitive church. The theory was not constructed on factual evidence but on a Hegelian mythology of history. Sir William Ramsay, who at first was taken in by the hypothesis, decided to test it out on the field in the Near East. The *facts* utterly changed his presuppositions. His research into the archeological data convinced him of Luke's reliability, and converted him to the authenticity of Acts.

The Gospel of John experienced a similar fortune at the hands of the critics. At first the work was taken to be a pious fiction, written by a well-meaning admirer of Jesus, but having no value as a historical source. The situation has entirely reversed itself today. It has been recognized that John is the most Jewish Gospel of the four and contains numerous details which suggest its author was an eyewitness. His accurate knowledge of Palestinian custom, history, and geography almost demand that the writer was himself a native of Palestine and a participant in the events he records.

These few examples show how precarious criticism of biblical infallibility is. For until the interpreter is omniscient and all the evidence comes in, it is impossible to press the theory of "inductive errancy." We ought neither to underestimate our task (for there remains much homework yet to be done), nor to overestimate its size (for it is nowhere nearly as large as the propaganda suggests). Difficulties in Scripture do not overthrow the infallibility principle. They are but mountains yet to be scaled and lands yet to be conquered.

XIII

THE LIVING GOD

The whole gospel message is grounded on one basic postulate: the existence of the sovereign triune God, who is both infinite and personal. Christian theology without this God is inconceivable to contemplate as geology without rocks or anthropology without man. Until recently the line was rather sharply drawn between atheism and theism at the point of God's existence. This is now no longer the case. Paul's principle of all things to all men has been extended to include the secular gospel. We are to address man in his secularity, and not require of him metaphysical beliefs foreign to his milieu. An ecumenical bridge has been thrown across the chasm of atheism and theism. Dialogue is encouraged between Christians and Marxists, Catholics and Buddhists, theists and humanists. Man and his concerns are so at the center of all contemporary thinking that God and his nature can be set aside as an indeterminate quantity. The rise to prominence of the theothanatologists (the "death-of-god" theologians) has only contributed to the ambiguity of his existence in the minds of many. The theoretical efforts of the theological morticians, together with the secular way of life today, combine to make the question a practical irrelevance.

Biblical religion approaches the question of God's existence from the angle of history. Its entire thrust arises from the claim that the living God has *shown himself* in historical events which cannot otherwise be explained than by acknowledging his existence. We have already noted how the new theology, whether it be existentialist or rationalistic, finds this aspect repugnant. Not enough certainty resides in history to support their conception of religion. The gospel notwithstanding does make her validity rest upon actual historical occurrences. The apostles did *not* witness to what God had done in the resurrection simply in order to indicate what God was doing in their lives. They appealed to the record of history because they believed it would yield evidence to the impartial observer of the truth of the gospel. The apostles had no wish to escape criticism on this score. They were convinced Jesus' rising was a plain fact, and did not fear close examination. For the Old and New Testaments, history is the medium in which revelation has unmistakably occurred. Faith and knowledge go hand in hand. Faith lays hold on the fact of Christ risen, and faces the future in the light of this. It is the structure of the biblical religion which determines its approach to the question of God's existence.

However, Scripture does not stop there. It does not suggest that those who have not been exposed to the light of historical revelation exist in some kind of theological limbo. On the contrary it boldly asserts that all men everywhere are always confronted with the fact of God's existence (Ps. 19:1; Rom. 1:18-25). It has been observed that nowhere does Scripture attempt a deductive argument for the existence of God like those of Thomas Aquinas for example. This fact ought not to be taken to imply, however, that such an effort is unjustifiable and necessarily useless. The distinctiveness of the biblical approach is its *immediacy*. The theistic proofs for God's existence constitute a laborious, painstaking, and patient justification of theism. They attempt to set forth in rational argument what the soul grasps intuitively. But for the Bible the deepest proof of God's existence is just life itself. The knowledge of God and man's knowledge of himself are closely intertwined. If only God could be written off neatly and cleanly, how simple things would be. But the hound of heaven pads after us all. He does not let us go. There is no escaping him. At the moment when least expected he closes in. The explanation for this is man's creation in the image of God (Gen. 1:26). His identity is known theologically, in relation to the God who is. Man in his true significance cannot survive permanently in isolation from his Maker. Without God man is the chance product of unthinking fate and of little worth. The current loss of identity and the emergence of the faceless man in today's culture is testimony to the effects of losing our God. The knowledge of God is given in the same movement in which we know ourselves.

Paul taught too that the natural order witnesses to the existence of an infinite personal God (Rom. 1:19f). The world is stamped with his trademark. It is an artifact constructed by an invisible craftsman. It is impossible, the apostle states, to avoid the conclusion that an almighty power exists apart from the visible order. Man's condition of low visibility is not due to the absence of evidence for God's existence, but to his own blindness, which is related to the sin problem. It is imperative to notice that Scripture *never* connects unbelief to the I.Q. or the lack of sound evidence; for there are reasons adequate for all. Unbelief is rather due to man's willful autonomy and refusal to bow before the living God. He is without excuse. The data present in the natural order which testifies to God's reality gets through to every man, but his reaction to it is conditioned by his state of soul. Because he is a covenant breaker and enemy of God (Rom. 8:7f; II Cor. 4:4), his receiving gear dulls, deflects, and perverts the testimony that comes. Though he is more an atheist in lip than life, he continues to resist the still small voice of God. He lives as if it were true, while denying it is so. It is difficult to live with the implications of the belief that in the beginning matter created the heavens and the earth, whether scientifically, philosophically, or morally. And he does not live with them, but daily cheats against his presuppositions. The world is not a mechanistic cage and man knows it. God speaks from within man's nature as created in the image of God and summons him back to the Father's house.

In Romans 2 Paul adds another pointer to God's existence within the consciousness of man. "Therefore you have no excuse, O man, whoever you are, when you judge another; for in passing judgment upon him you condemn yourself, because you, the judge, are doing the very same things" (v. 1). Paul does not claim here that all men have the same moral codes. They do not. Where man is his own lawgiver and where a moral warp exists in his soul, we could not expect the law of God to emerge unsullied in his systems of ethics. Paul merely claims that all men have moral *motions*. They set up standards of behavior, condemn others for not keeping to them, and turn around to violate them themselves. Man is condemned within the circle of his own consciousness. No man at the judgment can say, "I did not know." The divine tribunal sits in every human heart. The prominence of sacrifice in the religions of the world is proof of a guilty conscience and the desperate attempt to atone for sin. Men know their position before a holy God.

For the Scripture then, the existence of God is both a historical truth (God acted into history), and an existential truth (God reveals himself to every soul). His existence is both objectively and subjectively evident. It is necessary *logically* because our assumption of order, design, and rationality rests upon it. It is necessary *morally* because there is no explanation for the shape of morality apart from it. It is necessary *emotionally* because the human experience requires an immediate and ultimate environment. It is necessary *personally* because the exhaustion of all material possibilities still cannot give satisfaction to the heart. The deepest proof for God's existence apart from history is just life itself. God has created man in his image, and man cannot elude the implications of this fact. Everywhere their identity pursues them. Ultimately there is no escape. "Whither shall I go from thy Spirit? Or whither shall I flee from thy presence? If I ascend to heaven thou are there! If I make my bed in Sheol, thou art there!" (Ps. 139:7f).

XIV

THE GRAND MYTH

Every generation has its myths, and it is always easier to detect the myths of other cultures than our own. A myth is a story which offers an imaginary explanation for the origin and shape of life. So pervasively does it envelop the culture, and so exactly does it coincide with the contemporary spirit, that its inner absurdities go almost unnoticed. Anyone who would dare to dispute it is considered foolish. All educated people in the twelfth century knew the earth was flat. No other possibility was even considered. *Evolution* is the cultural myth of the twentieth century. It offers to provide a total explanation of all reality without requiring man to answer to the God of creation. It is religious to the core. Undoubtedly different lines of evidence are adduced which attempt to establish its factual basis, but these do not begin to explain the tenacity of the myth. Its pertinence to Christian apologetics is far deeper than is commonly admitted. Evolution in our day represents the attempt to furnish a total world view into which all reality will neatly fit. It places the whole phenomenal world, the realm of sense data, under the umbrella of naturalism, and leaves religion with the noumenal realm, the upper story, about which we can know nothing, but believe much. Since science is a sacred cow, we must tread softly. But it is imperative to insist that the attempt to ground reality in a naturalistic theory of origins *cannot* be done. It is impossible to assume in the light of current knowledge that order sprang out of bare chaos and life emerged spontaneously. Evolutionary dogmatism springs from religious a prioris and not from proven facts. On the contrary it imputes a bigger miracle to dead matter than the one creation requires. The root question to be answered is this: "Does creativity rest with God or Nature?" Has God ordained the decree in which all things work together (Eph. 1:11; Rom. 8:28) or has random chance through physical causation effected this? The choice is between Darwin's theory and the biblical God.

Almost every generation of men have believed themselves to be at the apex of knowledge. This makes the myths especially difficult to expose. Scientifically the concept of evolution has almost outworn its usefulness. So many inner contradictions have been pointed out that the hypothesis has ceased to be helpful. Yet the brainwashing goes on. High school textbooks, educational TV science programs, and the popular press continue to play on men's gullibility. Evolution (as if the term conveys a precise entity) is presented "as it happened." Charts and illustrations of life's progress over millions of years are shown. It would almost lead one to believe the magazine had live coverage! All of this despite the admitted fact that no scientist has come anywhere near demonstrating an unbroken line of evolution with any certainty. It is totally irresponsible to give the impression to students that evolution (whatever that means) is a demonstrated fact, or even a secure hypothesis. One can only conclude that the ruling intelligentsia have some motive for pushing this myth and converting our people to it. The motive is not difficult to discern. For the myth allows secular man to retain his autonomy without losing his freedom, or so they hope. Quite obviously the solution is not without non-scientific problems too. There is a severe tension between nature and freedom, as Hermann Dooyeweerd has pointed out. For a mechanical nature which runs on the lines of physical causation cannot easily become the mother of free and significant human beings. The two motifs clash with one another in a new form of the age-old paradox between freedom and determinism. But modern man needs his myth badly. Nature is his mother and her laws his principles, because he will not have God to reign over him. Yet freedom is his hope because otherwise he is a machine too. And so he is caught between two total and contradictory claims. Yet he prefers this tension to acknowledging the rights of the King. Indeed he sets up his own non-Christian upper and lower story. In the lower story he keeps his Nature with its omnipotent decree, and in the upper story he guards his pretended autonomy and religion. And despite the sheer irrationality of this structure that random selection should have produced freedom, order, and purpose, and that the entire event is one vast insurrection against the second law of thermodynamics, he hangs onto his precious myth. For freedom even in these chains is better, he thinks, than bondage to God.

Fundamentally evolution is an antiscientific myth. It is more a philosophy than a hypothesis. It makes man king at the top of the evolutionary pile, and promises him a nice man-made paradise at the end of the journey, an exquisite counterfeit of the biblical faith. But the myth is antiscientific. Dr. G. L. Jepsen, professor of vertebrate paleontology at Princeton University, remarked: "What we need are more competent fossils. We have plenty of competent anthropologists, but not nearly enough specimens. . . ." Much evolutionary thinking is entirely speculative and nonscientific. The current popularity of Teilhard de Chardin, with the backing of the high priest of the church scientific, Julian Huxley, is a case in point. His work is not successful because his facts are new or soundly based, but because the world is ready for the myth he projects. In fact, his entire theory of hominid history suffers from a whole series of missing links, and the proof for the grand hypothesis is almost totally lacking. Dr. William L. Strauss, Jr., professor of physical anthropology at Johns Hopkins University, commented, "the direct, or fossil, evidence for primate and hence for human evolution is relatively scanty and largely incomplete, too frequently consisting of mere fragments or even only teeth." Evolution succeeds not because it is a sound theory, but because it bolsters the humanistic faith which modern man has foolishly adopted in place of the Christian gospel. It persists despite nature, not because of her. But we face a church scientific whose propaganda has made even the truth sound strange. Evolution in its scientific aspects is a string on which data are suspended. With a fertile imagination and a little stretching, a case for it can be made out. But the harmony of the data with this theory exists largely in the mind of modern secular man who is blind to any other possibility. This is not a skirmish in the warfare between science and religion. Evolutionary science is as religious as religion is. If we jump on this bandwagon, we will do so not because the facts compel us, but because we want to. The real warfare between valid empirical science which stays within the field of legitimate inferences from data and which allows for the possibility of the biblical world view, and this pseudo science has scarcely begun. The assumption of the spontaneous origin of life is just about as reasonable as an explosion in a printing plant resulting in the twenty-four volumes of the *Encyclopedia Britannica*. The theory rests on inadequate factual grounds and there is reason for real doubt that it is a valid theory at all.

Sigmund Freud ran into one of the thorniest problems in evolution—genetics. As an atheist and naturalist, Freud was compelled to adopt the myth in some form. But he could not bring himself around to accepting the myth in its Darwinian version, because that involved natural selection. He felt that for natural selection to account for such a godlike creature as man was too big a miracle. So he admired Lamarck's theory of acquired characteristics until the end of his life, a fact which has embarrassed his biographers ever since. Lamarck offered him a possible mechanism for upward development which blind chance could not provide. However, Lamarck's hypothesis has been decisively disproven. Proficiency gained by the parent is not passed on to the child. Heredity depends upon gene chemistry, not intelligence. The fact of the matter is that genetics is opposed to *both* Darwin and Lamarck. For although micro-evolution can be observed within certain limits, this freedom is strictly controlled, and the genetic foundation between Darwin's theory of chance variations reproducing themselves is very weak if not nonexistent. The science of genetics has yet to supply a convincing explanation for the emergence of animal and plant groups. The example of Freud merely illustrates the dilemmas in and the confused state of current evolutionary thought. Every theory so far requires a miracle somewhere along the way greater than creation itself.

The myth is not without its tragic overtones, for it epitomizes the trapped position of man. In his self-understanding man is but the accidental product of blind chance. He is caught in an impersonal causal nexus. Chance and Fate are back of everything. There is no qualitative difference between man and a stone. Man is the most miserable creature in the universe, his identity lost, and his personality smothered by the weight of a "paneverythingism," in which the fittest, not the noblest, are the gods. Little wonder that he is seeking a return to chaos for salvation. For chaos, he believes, is the fountainhead of all reality, the source of all creativity and reality. Like the Saturnalia cult in ancient Rome, he desires a return to formlessness and lawlessness. He hopes that by negating law and order by violent revolution in every field he will find a paradise tomorrow. He derives his hope from his myth. But the hope

81

cannot materialize because reality is not this way. He is trapped in the horror of decreation, trusting in a myth which is scientifically dubious and philosophically nihilistic.

In America science is messianic. Scientists are priests and prophets of the current mythology. Often they speak as oracles of the new divinity. The problem this raises for Christians has little relation to actually demonstrated facts, but springs from a habit of thinking. The issue at bottom is the philosophy of science which today would play the role of infallible interpreter of all reality. Science is far from neutral. Evolution is her controlling concept, the framework which she assumes and within which she works. "What my net won't catch isn't fish." If this fact will not fit my theory, so much the worse for the fact! It represents a categorical denial of the biblical revelation. The theistic assertion of the gospel is exluded from the start. The only theory that will receive serious thought is one which can make peace with a naturalistic interpretation of the data. The Christian must be prepared to attack the basic presuppositions of current pseudo science, and insist that creativity rests with God, not nature. The Christian explanation of the origin of reality in the fiat creation of God deserves careful consideration. It frees the scientist from the need to provide an all-embracing theory of origins which his data simply will not sustain, and provides him with a stable world view in which his researches have solid foundations. But the Christian interpretation of reality is not an arbitrary, solipsistic hypothesis, like the interpretations of man. For, if Jesus Christ really rose from the grave, his interpretation of reality is certainly the correct one. The risen Christ is the focal point for all valid historical and scientific interpretation. "Where were you when I laid the foundation of the earth?" (Job 38:4; cf. Col. 1:16).

XV

A CONSISTENT APPROACH

"The Lord opened her heart to give heed to what was said by Paul" (Acts 16:14). Successful evangelism requires an inner and an outer event, the cooperation of a divine and a human witness. An evangelist must convey saving truth to the soul, and the Spirit must create the capacity to receive it. In saving men Jesus Christ employs two agents: the Holy Spirit in regeneration and conviction, and men in the presentation of the gospel. The outer testimony is used by the Spirit to create saving faith. He provides the inward confirmation that the message, understood intellectually, is true. Christian apologetics is concerned with the outer event, the role of the human witness. It goes almost without saying that apart from the work of the Spirit the gospel itself could only be truth on ice, cold and fruitless. The reason for this is traced back to the resistance of the natural man to the truth (Acts 7:51; I Cor. 2:14). The gospel itself, however, is solidly rooted in history and fact. It is our task to present a cogent testimony to its truthfulness.

Apologetic methodology ought to reflect faithfully and consistently a biblical theology. Man is finite and sinful. His reason is not ultimate in the universe. His mind is also fallen and twisted (Eph. 4:18). He needs both revelation for his finiteness and regeneration for his sinfulness. It will be forever impossible for man to explain the meaning of reality starting from himself alone. The Bible teaches that reality will not yield her secrets save on the basis of the Christian God and his revelation. Any other clue to the meaning of the universe is bound to prove frustrating and disappointing. Man's reason comes to real fruition when it acknowledges the self-revealing God and is regenerated. There can therefore be no naive presenting of the evidences for Christianity. A witness must be given and the data adduced, but the Spirit must be present to act upon the truth if it is to be effective. The problem in apologetics is not the

83

validity of the truth but its reception. The mind is like a sieve through which all the facts pass. They are sorted out in categories according to the shape of thought in the mind. The non-Christian interprets everything in accord with his naturalistic set of premises. Lumps of truth may get stuck in the sieve, but nothing will finally convert a person until the sieve itself is shattered.

This shattering in the last analysis is the work of the Spirit. The conviction of guilt, the radical unmasking of the sinner, is his task. "He will convince the world of sin" (Jn. 16:8). It is humanly impossible to do this. Yet there is a human role in the process of "elenctics." It is the role of prophetic preaching, the exposing of the gospel. For underneath all the argumentation and self-denial lies the basic sin of fleeing the living God. The negative side to apologetics, the radical unmasking, is part of the offense in evangelism. For it challenges the pretended autonomy of man-centered thinking. Man is not big enough to be his own *arche* (starting point). The fear of the Lord is the only *arche* of wisdom (Prov. 1:7). The non-Christian needs to be challenged to carry his starting point through in all his life and thinking if he can, and see where it leads him. It will lead him invariably to the breaking point. Meaning cannot be achieved apart from the gospel. "In Christ are hid all the treasures of wisdom and knowledge" (Col. 2:3). The whole structure derived from and depends on him. From the starting point of man's ultimacy and independence no progress can be made. Man cannot comprehend reality or himself from this point of departure. The finite mind cannot avoid a confession of bankruptcy. Any presentation of Christian evidences must be accompanied by a radical unmasking. There is no place in the universe for man to stand unless the Christian God exists.

According to an old tale, certain clever philosophers approached an emperor, offering to weave for him a rare and costly garment which would have the marvelous capacity of making known to him the fools and knaves in his realm. Because of the magic quality of the threads, the garment would be invisible to all but the wise and the pure in heart. Delighted, the emperor commissioned the weaving of the royal robes at great cost, only to find to his dismay, that he obviously was a fool and knave for he saw nothing on the looms. On the day set for the grand parade, the knavish philosophers collected their royal fee, dressed the emperor in his pot-bellied nakedness, and skipped out of town as the parade began. The whole populace joined the couriers in praising the king's garments, none daring to admit that they saw nothing but the emperor's nudity, lest they be branded as self-admitting fools and knaves. The entire parade of folly collapsed, as the shame of king and people was exposed by a child's honest remark, "The emperor has no clothes!"

The story has often been retold, with no small homilies on the feelings of king and people. But, significantly, the boy has been neglected, as truth usually is. Consider the future of that boy: with one small truth, he exposed a national and personal lie. With a grain of truth, he turned a people's glory into shame. It is no wonder nothing is said of him. The knavish philosophers got off scott free, and rich as well. Emperor and people went on with their everyday activities, eating, drinking, marrying and giving in marriage. But the small boy was to old age an outcast: he had told the truth and shamed his race. Not only the king's nakedness, but that of his people, even of his father and mother, had been exposed to the public gaze by his truth. None were consciously naked until this truth destroyed their lie, ripping away their fig-leaf of common hypocrisy (R. J. Rushdoony, *By What Standard*, 19f).

Everybody's pride was hurt. He could have broken the truth gradually and in pieces. He showed utter lack of tact. But that situation, and our own, calls for forthrightness, not diplomacy. According to the Bible the non-Christian positions are deceptive and self-defeating. It is high time for a prophetic voice to be raised in the name of Christ against the vanity of man-centered thinking and the need for intellectual repentance. Apologetics has been sleeping long enough, afraid of its own shadow and of a direct confrontation. "I have set before you life and death—choose life!" (Deut. 30:19).

All men employ the rational function. They are capable of receiving and evaluating data. Because of the noetic effects of sin, however, the non-Christian is unwilling to allow the truth of the gospel to have its persuasive effect in his life. The miracle of regeneration coincident with the presentation of the gospel is required in order to convert him to Christ. The faith which the Spirit creates in the heart is an intelligent faith, and we must fulfill our role of bringing to the attention of people the grounds of faith. For all men live in God's world and cannot succeed in their attempt to root all things back into chance. At some point they cheat, and live as if the gospel were true. Our strategy must be to stalk our prey, to plot his intellectual and moral position, and to close in with that which may heal his wounds and release him from captivity. The radical unmasking must take place.

There is a cafeteria of clues to the meaning of the universe. Men do adopt a set of presuppositions in order to sort out the avalanche of facts which confront them in reality. Often these premises are not examined. However, the history of ideas shows us clearly that great thinkers have frequently been known to exchange one set of presuppositions for another. In time it can become apparent that an earlier set of axioms no longer does the job and requires significant alteration. People are converted from one ideology to another daily. The non-Christian is operating on a naturalistic set of premises. Without the work of the Spirit he is unlikely to change them, not, however, because the Christian presuppositions are not truer and better in every way, but because he has no *will* to. Christian apologetics is called upon to challenge the validity of the non-Christian starting point, and to offer a far better one. God has broken into history in the person of Jesus Christ. The data are there for all to examine. We must challenge the non-Christian to suspend his prejudice against Christianity for the time it takes to examine fairly the evidence for the Christian faith, to take up a proven method for ascertaining truth, the empirical method, and apply it to the biblical records. No one is imprisoned within an iron cage of presuppositions. By the truth of the gospel and through the power of the Spirit he can be freed.

John Warwick Montgomery tells a revealing story in this connection.

> Once upon a time there was a man who thought he was dead. His concerned wife and friends sent him to the friendly neighbourhood psychiatrist. The psychiatrist determined to cure him by convincing him of one fact that contradicted his belief that he was dead. The psychiatrist decided to use the simple truth that dead men do not bleed. He put his patient to work reading medical texts, observing autopsies, etc. After weeks of effort, the patient finally said, "All right, all right! You've convinced me. Dead men do not bleed." Whereupon the psychiatrist stuck him in the arm with a needle, and the blood flowed. The man looked down with a contorted, ashen face and

cried: "Good Lord! Dead men bleed after all!" (*The Altizer-Montgomery Dialogue*, p. 21f).

Montgomery goes on to comment astutely:

> This parable illustrates that if you hold unsound presuppositions with sufficient tenacity, facts will make no difference at all, and you will be able to create a world of your own, totally unrelated to reality and totally incapable of being touched by reality. Such a condition (which the philosophers call solipsistic, psychiatrists call autistically psychotic, and lawyers call insane) is tantamount to death because connection with the living world is severed. The man in the parable not only thought he was dead, but in a very real sense, he *was* dead because facts no longer meant anything to him.

Undoubtedly such men exist for whom Christian evidences hold no interest or cogency. Until their own ship of state breaks up on the rocks of irrational absurdity, they will not open their ears to the good news. But the majority of men are not so. They still seek a haven of rest, not in the leap of ungrounded faith, but in commitment to the historical verities of the gospel.

CONCLUSION: THE EVANGELICAL IMPERATIVE

The decision of an intelligent man is based upon rational considerations. Choosing one's world view is not a game of Russian roulette. Our generation is sick of autobiographical theology in which nothing comes to the surface except personal prejudices. The root factor in the Christian message is its appeal to history. The destruction of historical objectivity and the elimination of the essential subject-object distinction has proved fatal to Christian apologetics. The counterattack must be on a wide front. Faith which floats around in a sea of untestable assertions is empty and deceptive. The purpose of apologetics is to remove prejudice against the gospel and to lay a solid basis for faith in it. People are constantly affected in their actions and choices by arguments, intelligent or otherwise. The notion that nobody is ever converted to Christ by argument is a foolish platitude. It would be more accurate to say that the reason so few are being converted to him now, is because so many Christians believe the fallacy. It is high time for us to restock the arsenal of Christian evidences, and confront our contemporaries with a solid message. Christians who are addicted to the existential divorce from reality are lazy witnesses. In a world which is increasingly alienated from the body of divine revelation, a "faith in faith" solution will not meet the need, and sinners will not hear the gospel. The hour has struck for a renaissance in Christian letters, and the training of a body of articulate apologists. We need a group of well-trained scholars capable of following the myths of our day to their source, and exposing them there. Their ministry would include travelling from city to city, and university to university, defending the whole faith and presenting the evidence for its validity. Out of their midst would come a library of new literature in every area of theological concern, which would spark a revival in life and truth throughout the length and breadth of the Christian Church. Ours is a day of specialization. Men are preoccupied with the minutiae in science and history. We sadly lack men who understand the broad sweep of the contemporary intellectual climate, and who can relate the gospel intelligently to it. To do this, the boundary lines between various disciplines must be crossed bravely, and the connections drawn which illuminate the entire field of human thought. Until this is done, our apologetics will be piecemeal and unconvincing.

The usefulness of Christian apologetics goes far beyond evangelism and personal soul winning. It also fills the believer's heart with joy as he contemplates the factuality and truth of his faith. What an encouragement to know with mind and emotions that our salvation is grounded in objective reality! Christianity is a historical religion. Evidences are therefore important to it. They do not convert the soul; they do distinguish faith from mere gullibility. This places a heavy weight of responsibility upon the shoulders of educated Christians. For they have a ministry to the whole Church of demonstrating that the ground of its faith is sound. This aspect of the gift of teaching has been sadly lacking in the body of Christ for some time now. The moment has come to revive this gift within our midst and place much strenuous effort behind the defense of the faith. For besides being a potent weapon in our evangelistic thrust, it is the life preserver that can rescue our Christian young people drowning in the sea of uncertainty. The beauty of the gospel is its facticity. But professing it, and demonstrating it publicly are two different things. Conservative Christians have failed to do their homework. We have left the critical fields of philosophy, history, anthropology, and the social sciences to biblically uncommitted and even anti-Christian scholarship. The results of this surrender are proving catastrophic. Nothing short of a Christian reformation can alter the direction of the stream. But the change must be brought about. But, it will not be done without sweat and tears. Prooftexts and slogans will arouse the saints but will not win the battle. If the Christian gospel is to regain a position of authority in shaping the form of our culture, a great deal of hard work is ahead for us. To fight the good fight of faith requires a good deal more intellectual sinews and muscles than most Christians realize.

The apostle Paul explained his strategy for personal evangelism in the words "all things to all men" (I Cor. 9:22). He meant to imply nothing of the modern notion of relativism which today would be attached to such a slogan. His faith in the historical truthfulness and doctrinal content of the gospel is well known. His emphasis lay in another direction. Effective evangelism requires a personal accommodation without compromise of truth to the total situation of men. In his own life Paul showed tremendous versatility getting alongside people from various backgrounds. He was able to communicate the data of the gospel with maximum effect because he showed himself willing to understand his audience. To the slave he became a slave, to the Jew a Jew, to the Roman a Roman. His strategy of personal empathy and understanding is relevant today. We need to make a conscious effort to comprehend the darkness outside of Christ. A complacent, bourgeois church cannot do this. The agony and tears of the secular prophets must be shared if we are to convince them of the pertinence of the gospel. Our age is vastly overrated. The common opinion that man has come of age is contrary to all empirical tests except the advance in technology which may yet destroy us all. Morally and spiritually man is still an infant. Historic Christianity can be effectively preached in the twentieth century. The new theologies will pass away because they seek to rescue the perishing by sinking the lifeboat. Yet the biblical faith will not gain a hearing in our culture until Christians shake off their cultural apathy and engage themselves in the debates of our time. Nor is it a matter only of accommodation to the intellectual and spiritual currents of our day. There needs to be a personal and corporate demonstration in the Church of the existence of God and the truth of the gospel. The Christian life is posited upon the reality of biblical truth. The normal Christian life ought to contain powerful proofs for the gospel in the form of answered prayer and clear direction. Too much of orthodox Protestantism is spiritually dead. It trusts as much in carnal methods and procedures as men of the world do. Small wonder men have not found its message credible. Our evidence will not be accepted so long as our lives are not authentic. The greatest hindrance to the spread of the gospel is the shallowness of Christians. Men are deterred from considering Christ because our lives are unreal and false. God's men for this hour must be transparently genuine, committed, and convinced.

The task of Christian apologetics is a serious one. Let no one take it on without realizing the issues. For while it can be life unto life, it can also be death unto death (II Cor. 2:14). When the Pharisees were confronted with unmistakable proofs of Jesus' divinity, they hardened their hearts further, and blasphemed against the Holy Spirit (Mt. 12:22-32). Jesus himself warned that an awareness of his person and work increases the responsibility of men regarding their spiritual position (Jn. 15:24). It is a sobering thought to recognize the tragic results that can ensue from effective apologetics. "If anyone comes to me and does not hate even his own life, he cannot be my disciple" (Lk. 14:26). The cost of discipleship to Jesus Christ is dear in the field of apologetics. It will be measured in hours of exhausting discussion, in harsh words of studied contempt, in personal inconvenience and discomfort. But he who said, "You shall be witness unto me" also said, "Lo, I am with you always, even unto the end of the age."

A SELECTIVE BIBLIOGRAPHY
ON CHRISTIAN APOLOGETICS

Babbage, Stuart, *The Mark of Cain*, Eerdmans, 1966.

Bruce, F. F., *Are the New Testament Documents Reliable*, Inter-Varsity Fellowship, 1943.

————, *The Apostolic Defense of the Gospel*, Inter-Varsity Fellowship, 1959.

Carnell, E. J., *An Introduction to Christian Apologetics*, Eerdmans, 1956.

————, *A Philosophy of the Christian Religion*, Eerdmans, 1952.

Clark, Gordon, *A Christian View of Men and Things*, Eerdmans, 1952.

Dooyeweerd, H., *A New Critique of Theoretical Thought*, 4 volumes, Presbyterian and Reformed Publishing Company, 1953-58.

————, *In the Twilight of Western Thought*, Presbyterian and Reformed Publishing Company, 1960.

Freeman, David H., *Recent Studies in Philosophy and Theology*, Presbyterian and Reformed Publishing Company, 1962.

————, editor, *Modern Thinkers Series*, Presbyterian and Reformed Publishing Company.

Fuller, Daniel P., *Easter Faith and History*, Eerdmans, 1965.

Gerstner, John H., *Reasons for Faith*, Harper & Row, n.d.

Hamilton, Floyd E., *The Basis of Christian Faith*, G. H. Doran Co., 1927.

Henry, Carl F. H., *Remaking the Modern Mind*, 2nd ed., Eerdmans, 1948.

————, *Giving a Reason for Our Hope*, W. A. Wilde, 1949.

Lewis, C. S., *Mere Christianity*, Collins, 1952.

————, *Miracles*, Collins, 1947.

Lightner, Paul, *The Saviour and Scriptures*, Presbyterian and Reformed Publishing Company, 1965.

Little, Paul E., *How to Give Away Your Faith*, Inter-Varsity Press, 1966.

MacGregor, James, *Studies in the History of Christian Apologetics*, T & T Clark, 1894.

Montgomery, John W., *The Shape of the Past*, Edwards Brothers, Inc., 1962.

————, *The 'Is God Dead' Controversy*, Zondervan, 1966.

————, "History and Christianity," *HIS* magazine, offprint.

————, "The Place of Reason," *HIS*, Feb. and March, 1966.

Morrison, Frank, *Who Moved the Stone?*, Faber and Faber, 1958.

Mullins, E. Y., *Why Is Christianity True*, American Baptist Publication Society, 1911.

Orr, James, *The Christian View of God and the World*, Scribner, 1897.

Phillips, J. B., *Ring of Truth*, Macmillan, 1967.

Pinnock, Clark H., *A Defense of Biblical Infallibility*, Presbyterian and Reformed Publishing Company, 1967.

Ramm, Bernard, *Protestant Christian Evidences*, Moody Press, 1957.

——, *Varieties of Christian Apologetics*, Baker, 1961.

Richardson, Alan, *Christian Apologetics*, SCM Press, 1947.

——, *History Sacred and Profane*, SCM Press, 1964.

Rushdoony, Rousas J., *By What Standard?*, Presbyterian and Reformed Publishing Company, 1959.

——, *Intellectual Schizophrenia*, Presbyterian and Reformed Publishing Company, 1961.

——, *The Messianic Character of American Education*, Craig Press, 1963.

——, *The Mythology of Science*, Craig Press, 1967.

Shute, Evan, *Flaws in Evolution*, Craig Press, 1961.

Smith, Wilbur M., *Therefore Stand*, W. A. Wilde, 1945.

Stott, John R. W., *Basic Christianity*, Inter-Varsity Press, 1958.

Van Til, Cornelius, *Defense of the Faith*, Presbyterian and Reformed Publishing Company, 1955.

——, *Is God Dead?*, Presbyterian and Reformed Publishing Company, 1966.

Yamauchi, Edwin, *Composition and Corroboration in Classical and Biblical Studies*, Presbyterian and Reformed Publishing Company, 1966.